Praise for
Gravity Prevails

Deeply aware of the centuries-old history, geography, and culture of the land spanning Texas and Mexico, Kamala Platt offers in *Gravity Prevails* the richness of re-memories of this living, breathing colonized geography that continues to nurture its inhabitants, human, animal, and flora. In rich lyricism, sonorous with Spanish, Indian and English languages, the poet hears men and women from the past, echoed by seedlings calling the names of the living and the departed. We are woken up to recognize the plants and the birds that make our lives beautiful but whose lives have become more and more precarious in our "civilization" with its "man-generated climate change." Will nature continue to prevail? Egrets return even when they are displaced, but some plants are unable to return when we destroy the soil. Kamala feels with the earth. She writes, "Gardeners work with the soil….a living ecosystem," cognizant of the body's dance with the earth, listening to its heartbeat and learning from it how to live. Kamala's *Gravity Prevails* is an urgent plea to us to pay attention to our injustice toward indigenous and marginalized people, to the planet itself, and, therefore, live life protecting Earth mother, Pachamama, who protects us. This volume is essential reading for anyone with a conscience.

— **Pramila Venkateswaran**, poet laureate of Suffolk County, NY, and author of *The Singer of Alleppey* (Shanti Arts, 2018)

The poems in *Gravity Prevails* are both soothing and explosive as the poet searches for harmony and common ground. While consistently critical of the violence men have wrought against life, Platt is also sensitive to the beauty and power found in the diversity of differences. These poems pay homage to the intimacy of neighbors and the struggle for peace, justice and community endurance. Intent on writing wrongs, this collection serves as a healing balm. Expressing a fierce urgency, these paeans are also prayers, chants, curses, and rebellious gritos thrown, at times, in rage, but always infused with love.

— **Dr. Louis Mendoza**, Director School of Humanities, Arts, and Cultural Studies at Arizona State University

Kamala Platt's important new book of poems, *Gravity Prevails*, brings together her activism, her commitment to environmental justice and indigenous rights, her life in Kansas and San Antonio, travels, work, local flora, homage to social justice leaders, artists and neighbors. She has an ear and an eye for pain and rights violated, but marks that suffering with grace, humor, dignity, and deep reflection. She offers a multi-lingual, richly textured dance, dedication that reaches our hearts and feet: "In Kansas there is a Mennonite joke/that says we forbid sex because it might lead to dancing/And yes, dancing is that basic— as the First Peoples tell it: Dance is the heartbeat of Nuestra Madre/ red mud trembling, universal frenzy made fuerza unida."

— **Cheryl J. Fish**, author of *Crater & Tower*, and *The Sauna is Full of Maids*

Kamala wanders like a migrant from state to state, from region to region, from culture to culture, from issue to issue, electrifying us with what she sees and feels and thinks. She weaves her words in her poems so that each poem stands alone in its reckonings. Her poem, beginning with the words "Shovel It", goes to my heart because it identifies where we should go, where we should be in terms of the environment because this is what she and many of us stand for and she puts her words together so eloquently, so basically. We can identify. And then she lives by her words.

— **Rebecca Flores**, friend and fellow traveler

The world is too much with us, and too often, we cannot see beyond it. For Mexicans in Texas, the world has always been such, but we have resisted con ganas, lessons imparted in these beautiful writings by Kamala Platt. Like some Dorothy from Kansas, she came as a woman to craft her message of hope and struggle in Texas. There is even a Toto, named Chato, that her San Antonio Westside neighborhood loves and protects because he "spread goodwill to all." Love and goodwill but also passionate struggle are what Kamala offers in this work even as her love reaches back to her ancestral Kansas and her parents and beyond in her "letter to the world." Back on the Westside, conjunto music disappears, but she and her neighbors share berries and flowers, "no charge." Here gravity will not prevail. Kamala lifts us to see the world as it might be.

— **José E. Limón**, Mody C. Boatright Regents Professor of American Literature University of Texas at Austin (Emeritus)

GRAVITY PREVAILS

FLOWERSONG
PRESS

poems by
Kamala Platt

FLOWERSONG
PRESS

FlowerSong Press
Copyright © 2022 by Kamala Platt
ISBN: 978-1-953447-41-8
Library of Congress Control Number: 2021952738

Published by FlowerSong Press
in the United States of America.
www.flowersongpress.com

Cover Image: Gulf Fritillary on Amaranth by Kamala Platt
Author Photo by Margie Hildebrand
Cover Art Design by Kamala Platt
Set in Adobe Garamond Pro

No part of this book may be reproduced without
written permission from the Publisher.

All inquiries and permission requests should
be addressed to the Publisher.

NOTICE: SCHOOLS AND BUSINESSES
FlowerSong Press offers copies of this book at quantity discount with bulk purchase for educational and business use. For information, please email the Publisher at info@flowersongpress.com.

To all my animals and plantitas and to *letting them grow as they will…*

Introduction

Sometimes I had felt compelled to take some action which I thought might help lead to peace, but I had held back because I did not want to seem conspicuous. . . Now when I see an issue to which my life should speak, I think of my children, and I try to break the pattern of generations that holds me back. In doing what I can as a parent, I pray that the cycle of life for my children may continue and that the new pattern may be woven into a world of peace.

— LaVonne Platt, 1967

The title of this collection came to me as an act of desperation, an admittance that life was subject to universal principles I had barely taken note of, though I was aware they were as present in my life as my breathing. They were as hidden as that systemic pulsing, originating in a throbbing heart embedded in a nurturing biome and protective skin. I had paid attention to gravity both literally and figuratively, in a simplistic way—as that nuisance force at play when things fell off or over or got me down. I realized I had to acknowledge that gravity's force also kept things in place—its force was basic to our not floating off, to our state of existence. In that sense, in my mind, gravity became a stand-in word for art. How so?

My mother 's reading voice was near perfect to me—an astute ability I wish I had inherited. From stories before bedtime that are among my earliest memories to her reading from her own writing at my request, in her last years, —she had a consistently- dynamic reading voice paired with the authenticity of honest connection that compelled the listener to "hear" even after her other linguistic skills were failing her. At the end of a poetry reading I gave for my home community at the Meadowlark Center the summer after Wings Press published *On the Line*, my mom came up to me, very excited. "I could hear you. I could hear just about everything." she exclaimed. She meant it literally, though perhaps figuratively, as well. We knew that treating her increasing hearing loss and beginning dementia was more complicated, and more basic, than obtaining expensive, new-fangled hearing aids and doing sudoku puzzles—her hearing my reading was a breakthrough interlude I thought about many times, afterward. Had we witnessed the ancient power of poetry-read-aloud, manifested? Was the emotional connection to her daughter's words what moved her mind to again hear clearly? Could we have somehow sustained that interlude? Through words, art, synapse, or some force of nature? I follow a similar line of questioning when thinking about how to find a "new pattern that may be woven into a world of peace" in a world with an increasingly discombobulating climate—in all senses of the word.

I wrote this collection over the last twenty years and the range of subject, languages and genres may seem haphazard to some. Some of it may be of what Ana Castillo in *I Ask the Impossible* calls "pertaining to no-school-that-I-know-of brand of poetry." For me, writing poems has something in common with propagating plants—we cast seed or cut slips, or transplant pups or merely nourish dormant land into conditions that we believe will nurture growth. When the work brings response, we know something is up and growing inside, maybe even beginning to bud. When it "connects" out in the world we've got roots. When, despite all odds, someone "hears" it, we know that insects are buzzing around it, and likely bigger animals and birds and smaller microbes are nearby. We work to make our relationships the best they can be: our planting has birthed ecosystem and poetry has found community.

Acknowledgements

My great, great gratitude to everyone (family, friends, students, mentors, neighbors, and those who are all of the above), named in these pages or not, whose good energy and words and deeds inspired the poetry and went into "making something" as Cecile Pineda calls creative process in *Three Tides: Writing as the Edge of Being*; that "something" became this book. I am especially grateful for those I've read with and listened with on Zoom, these last many months, and for earlier gatherings of Stone in the Stream, Roca en El Rio. My thanks goes out to fellow travellers, soulmates, allies to la lucha, those who people my poems and my life with respect and kindness, including those I have lost touch with and those among us who have died. In my poems to my mother, I am remembering all of you who are still with us in memories.

This collection of poems was gestated within a pandemic. The last large public-in person-gathering I attended last year (at the invitation of Gemini Ink (to whom I will be forever grateful) was the AWP, (Association of Writers & Writing Programs) in San Antonio, in early March of 2020. The reunions and new friends made, the readings, inspiration, concerns, discussions, comida and abrazos shared, there, have kept me going until now. The story of *Gravity Prevails* began at the Perugia Press booth, where I met and chatted with Rebecca Olander. She told me about their one publication a year—a first or second poetry book from a woman poet whose manuscript won their contest. I decided then and there that I would gather my poetry into a book for this contest. The last AWP-related event I attended was an evening reception where I fondly remember eating multiple helpings of wonderful comida and chatting with folks from El Valle. I remember Edward Vidaurre suggesting I send work to FlowerSong Press. I must have smiled because I felt sure then that the book I would put together would have a home. The turn-around time between Perugia's rejection email one afternoon last March (they read over 500 manuscripts) and Flower Song's acceptance email was just over two hours. Muchísimas gracias to Edward Vidaurre and all who "nurture verse" at FlowerSong Press-- your borderland work is truly "essential." Birthing this book has been painless, even in these hard, hard times. As someone who identifies as a "world citizen," becoming part of a borderland press family that serves the world is more than I had dreamed of.

My parents have been my best readers providing both support and critical response for my work since childhood. I turned to my dad, Dwight Platt, when I was putting together the manuscript for Perugia, and he provided a much-needed second pair of eyes, an ecologist's wisdom, gardening know-how and a reader's consternation at points where more work was needed.

My thanks to the Garden of Good Trouble for the Gulf Fritillary and amaranth that grace the cover of *Gravity Prevails* and to Edward and Mary Agnes Rodriguez for helping me get the colors and shapes of the letters just right.

My deep appreciation to those who wrote kind and discerning words for blurbs—you have honored my wordwork, humbled me, and even made me laugh.

Thank you's to the editors of publications who have previously published some of the poems (often in earlier versions) in this collection. Most extensively, this includes my appreciation to Finishing Line Press, which published my chapbook *Weedslovers: Ten Years in the Shadow of September*, (Poetry) in March 2014.

Other publications include:

"Something, Ending" & "Egrets' Elegies " in *Boundless 2021: the anthology of the Rio Grande Valley International Poetry Festival.* Edward Vidaurre, Sarah Joy Thompson, Gabriel González, Eds.

"Pandemic is a Place Where Harassing Migratory Birds is Essential Business #1" & "Found Poem: Border Wall Public Comments" *Life and Legends* Issue no 10. Kalpna Singh-Chitnis, Lopamudra Banerjee, Megha Sood, & Nirvan Chitnis, Eds.
lifeandlegends.com/poetry-kamala-platt/

"Rio Grande/ Bravo Watershed…" in *Odes and Elegies: Eco-Poetry from the Texas Gulf Coast.* Katherine Hoerth, Ed. Lamar University Press, 2020.
https://www.lamar.edu/literary-press/poetry/odes-and-elegies-eco-poetry-from-the-texas-gulf-coast.html

"Lines from Inside a Pandemic" (eight poems) in *No Season for Silence: Texas Poets and Pandemic* Milton Jordan, Ed., Kallisto Gaia Press Inc., 2020.
https://www.kallistogaiapress.org/product/no-season-for-silence-texas-poets-and-pandemic/

"Ardeidae Anthem" & "Letting them grow as they will: prairie synthesis and sustenance Father-Daughter Correspondence Found Poem" with Dwight Platt, *Voices de la Luna: A Quarterly Literature & Arts Magazine*, Special Earthday Issue, February 2020.

"'La Posta del Palo Alto' as San Antonio Poeta, 1935" in *30 Poems for the Tricentennial: A Poetic Legacy*. CoSA Dept. of Arts & Culture & Gemini Ink, San Antonio's Literary Arts Center, chapbook publication and exhibit 30 Poems for the Tricentennial: A Poetic Legacy, November 15, 2018- April 25, 2019. Plaza de Armas, San Antonio, TX. http://events.getcreativesanantonio.com/event/detail/442024508/30_Poems_for_the_Tricentennial_A_Poetic_Legacy

"Art Is…Manifesto" and "City of Tiny Terrors" in *Tuesday Night Live: A Gathering of Curley's Poets*, Turn of River Press, 2018.
http://www.yuganta.com/turn-of-river-press/tuesday-night-live/

"City of Tiny Terrors" in *This City is A Poem*, April 2018
https://thiscityisapoem.tumblr.com/post/173408056922/city-of-tiny-terrors

"Wilding in San Antonio" *About Place* literary journal, Black Earth Institute, "Rewilding Urban Life" Vol.V. Issue I.,
https://aboutplacejournal.org/issues/rewilding/rewilding-urban-life/kamala-platt/

"Resistance Plantings at Hay's Street Bridge People's Park" (August, 2017); "Epistle del Amor: Love Letter to My City (January, 2016) in "*Voices de la Luna: A Quarterly Literature & Arts Magazine*, May 2016, Roca en El Río/ Stone in the Stream page: http://voicesdelaluna.org

"What Gravity Reveals" in *Connective Tissue: Literature & Visual Arts Journal*, UTHSCSA p 40-41. 2016.
https://issuu.com/uthscsacmhe/docs/ct_2016_issue_final

"Notes on Envelope: Found Poem from Mt. Zion's Nelson Mandela Tribute, San Antonio TX" in *Pushing the Envelope: Epistolary Poems*. Jonas Zdanys, Ed., Lamar University Press, 2015.
http://www.lamaruniversitypress.org/resources/PressRelease-Pushing-Envelope.pdf

"'Glimpse: a fable for our common future," "Saturday's Synchronicity II," & "Bound" in *THE POETRY OF RESISTANCE: 33 CONTEMPORARY AMERICAN VOICES*. Fred Whitehead, Ed., Kansas City, KS: John Brown Press, 2014.

"Emigrantes Ambientales" Trilogy in *SSGA El Mundo Zurdo II Proceedings* Aunt Lute Books (San Francisco) 2012.

"Mary's Gift" & "Seasonal Still Life 2011" (2014) "Kali's Calavera" (2009) in *La Voz de Esperanza*, publication of the Esperanza Peace & Justice Center, San Antonio, TX. https://esperanzacenter.org/la-voz/

"Emigrantes Ambientales I & III" in *Boundless* 2010 (May, 2010).

"Dancing for La Gloria" in *Tonatzin*, Guadalupe Cultural Arts (Conjunto Festival Pub. May 2009).

"Viaje Into the Vortex" in *The Beatest State in the Nation: An Anthology of Beat Texas Writing*, Christopher Carmona, Rob Johnson, Chuck Taylor, Eds. Beaumont, TX: Lamar University Literary Press, 2016.

"Anglicized" in *Kinientos: New Picture of an Old World*, Wordsworth, 1992.

Contents

I. Origins

Anglicized......2
'La Posta' as Una San Antonio Poeta, 1935......3
Weedslover......5
Estero Llano Grande......6

II. Meadowlark Chronicles

Viaje Into the Vortex......8
Seasonal Still Life, September 2011......9
One recipe you cannot google—yet......10
Letting them grow as they will:
finding prairie synthesis and sustenance......12

III. Westside San Antonio

Mary's gift (*From Meadowlark to Martin Street*)......16
Conjunto: Dancing for La Gloria I & II......17
Westside Gardens: No Charge......19
Day after Día de Los Muertos at the Rinconcito......20

IV. Por La Paz

Questions for Wantin' Times n' Wa-rrr-in' Times
and an Answer (Out) of Sorts......22
Eagle Ford Shale: A Free Form Fracking Corrido-Sonnet......25
Notes on Envelope: Found Poem from Mt. Zion's
Nelson Mandela Tribute......27
Art is…Manifesto......29

V. Coahuiltecan's Lands

Borderland Trilogy in Four Stanzas......32
Kali's Calavera......33
April Litany of Fools' Waivers: An Elegy
Found In the Words of the Secretary of "Homeland Security"
with Greek Chorus......34
Epilogue to the Elegy for Poetry Month......37
Found Poem: Border Wall Public Comments, Fall, 07......38
Bound......40
Saturday's Synchronicity II, October 1, 2011......42
These are Ours......43
Rio Grande/ Bravo Watershed, 2018......45
Emigrantes Ambientales I: After Fallout......46
Emigrantes Ambientales II: Valles y Salud......47
Emigrantes Ambientales III Paddling Together......48
Glimpse: a fable for our common future......49

VI. Payaya People's Home

City of Tiny Terrors......54
Resistance Plantings at Hay's Street Bridge People's Park......56
HDRC TESTIMONY......57
What Gravity Reveals......59
Epistle del Amor......62

VII. Maternal Inheritance in Times of Great, Great Hate

Contemplating Complexity......64
Epistle, Friday, January 13th, 2017......68
For My Mother......70
Postscript: February,......72
La Despedida, The Sendoff, May 27, 2018......73

VIII. Westside Atzlan

Ardeidae Anthem......78
Egrets' Elegies
    I. Winter of Westside Displacement......80
    II. Essential Business......83

IX. Inside a Pandemic

Facebook Memorial, posted March 12, 2020......88
An Abundance of Wisdom......90
Rationing, Rationalizing, Pandemic Panic.....91
Decree......93
Social Bubbling......94
Meadowlark: Phone Notes......96
My Diary (Yet to be Named):
Found Poem in Pandemic......97
"Honk, it's my birthday!"......99

X. Impending

Volatilities......102
Flamenco for the Earth......104
Something, Ending......105
Mother Earth Pursues America's 19th Amendment......106

may we not change the emotion that guides us from that of fear to that of love?

— **LaVonne Godwin Platt**

…I humbly wish for y'all, un mundo in Peace.

— **raúl el poeta/ raúlrsalinas**

I. Origins

Anglicized

The languages of my ancestors
would be at least seven,
only one of which I know well.
Five are silent within me,
perhaps more—
Lost to earlier colonizers,
Hidden by the whiteness of my talk.
Mother tongues are imbedded
within us, like our mothers' names,
like our families' names—
Anglicized, made into angels.

Only when money talks, have we listened.
For the last 500 years
it has been speaking English here.
On these grounds
we must learn our dead languages
Learn to talk to each other
in our dead languages
Learn to talk to the dead within
Learn to listen for that which money has no words.

"La Posta" as una San Antonio Poeta, 1935
(after Elena Zamora O'Shea's novel, *El Mesquite*)

"[*El Mesquite's*] *pedagogical project of recovery, revision and reconciliation documents not the disappearance of indigenous peoples, but the persistence of indigeneity in the multiply-colonized, transnational geography of South Texas*"
— Kirby Brown

I was born Mizquitl
decades after deep soil first cuddled my mother's seed
dropped on the edge of this land of springs and caves,
not far from the stony rift where the coastal plains meet hill country,
in what is now the Westside of this city.

I was born Mizquitl
though I would soon hear my name mispronounced:
Mesquite, to Spanish expeditions of colonization.
The Anglos that followed spelled my name in strange ways:
mesquit, musquit, mezquit, musket, musket? —
Were these just mistakes,
or did they plan to use my wood for their guns?

I no longer recall all the ways my human comrades
called out to me, but many spoke
without the respect due to my Nahuatl birth name
that came from those in the south of our continent.

I was born Mizquitl—my roots go deep here—
over 100 feet of Westside loam.
My years go back in scores now—
more than 200 years.
Since before my birth,
peoples have crisscrossed our city
coming and going like the birds and butterflies
though in recent decades,
groups come through
without the reasons of the seasons.
Nor do many gather anymore
in the wisdom and spirit of the land
sitting and talking beneath my branches.

There has been talk since the cusp of the millennium
that scientists are discovering what my sister trees
and some sister humans too, already knew:
they say the seasons are getting feverish
and the waters have been taken in
by our own fickle ways and are leaving us dry.
Yet the women that pick open the pecans from my primas—
for the big companies, they rest from their weariness
in my shade as they walk home from work. They feed and
heal their families with my comida & medicine.
They are going to rise up in resistencia soon—
Their weariness will turn to revolt and all of earth herself—
we will all, be the better for it.

I was born Mizquitl
and I waited decades in the earth for the right conditions for my birth.
I am waiting now for the right conditions for our earth
to give life to the hope of the women of San Antonio.

Weedslover

The Cheyenne word is lost
to time's chasm--

stretching,
        spiraling in my mind.

"Weedslover"
is the imperfect translation
they gave, when
they named me,
who had but one name, as we—
all still young—
walked the ditches
of Hammond, Oklahoma

looking for nothing
        in particular,

and everything
        of color
                and calm
to exclaim over.

Estero Llano Grande

Big wet gathering spot on the dry plain
donde monte meets prairie,
coastal plains greet ebony,
and sabal, huisache, mesquite
host those travelers
who know México, Estados Unidos, Canadá are one.
Place of rest alongside the long mid-continental prairie
running south—from glaciers to gulf waters.

Place where I met all my kin…
two legged, four-legged, winged, finned & scaled.

Place where I heard seedlings
calling my names—
       Place of migration.
              Place of return.

II. Meadowlark Chronicles

Viaje Into the Vortex
Epistolary Poem to Allen Ginsberg

You traveled the highway above Meadowlark in '66
and wrote conservative Kansas back into a poetry against wars.
Now, that landscape is twice burned,
once by drought that would bond us to refugees of the earth's rising fever,
were we to ever leave our AC-befuddled rooms.

Your bus-trips probably passed by Leavenworth
where Raúl would be writing, reading, listening to languages
that lurk in the crevasses,
where wise ones chew cuds, masticate their palabras,
digest their comidas, build strength before being walled off
by the mean spirits metastasizing across the good earth, herself.

You traveled across Kansas
to proclaim Sutras against the wars
that began before my birth.

Before the fires began that summer,
I traveled back up
from the junction
of the Rio Grande de Bravo & the Chisholm Trail
following hoof-prints petrified into asphalt,
from where now a wall shuts us off
from the México the Beats loved.
Where they loved.
Where they immigrated to work
returning to the Magic Valle with palabras
that proclaim Sutras against those reoccurring wars,
the consumption we now *worship* with our day's work.

   p.s. I heard at the Peabody Farmer's Market
      that Florence, Kansas
         has no more pure spring water in its tower with which to make tea.

Seasonal Still Life, September 2011

"I cannot hear you speak but your letters take me to the far reaches of the world."*
— Troy Davis

Today, there were piles of feathers and a detached wing
outside the Meadowlark aviary where we found the peachicks,
their small bodies torn asunder.

Marauders—probably raccoons, maybe babies themselves,
followed drought-driven hunger that took them away
from the remnant of a stream, never before ephemeral,
where "fishlings" no longer squirmed in the mud.

It was the last day of summer.
105 degrees had reduced to 95 at midday and 75 at night
in Los Ebanos, Roma, Rio Grande where more walls
will be built on flood plains, homes will be evacuated,
and young animals will die
even if autumn rains ever come, again.
Yet, tonight, fires still smolder
& Atlokoya, goddess of drought, reigns,
though the peachicks' remains look more
like the dismembered Coyolhauhqui.

And tonight, the last day of summer,
at 11:08, their time,
the lights went out again in Georgia.

Tonight, despite the chanting that connected
the continents in the light of prayer and goodwill
Troy Davis was executed.

On this last day of summer,
he refused his last supper,
in order to spend time with his friends.

*Troy Davis' words come from his final letter to supporters
that I read in *Information Clearing House*, September 22nd, 2011.

One recipe you cannot google—yet

Blackberries from the Sand Hills—
the raccoons inadvertently led us to them
and memories of Mary's jam led us back
to pick them in July's steamy sun—small and sweet.
I froze them in cleaned (twice) ice cream cartons.

Blackberries from Meadowlark
transplanted plumpness swollen, pregnant
(like Raven the cat) with sour juice intact around the seed
frozen on trays and popped into freezer jars,
bygone wise ways rejuvenated:

August birthdays, Dog Days, Canícula, Local-food church potluck—
and all the blackberries, wild, wet with frost,
joined with honey—prairie grazed,
and labneh, not local, but it should be,
Kansas hard winter wheat germ crust
and Lidia's luminous berry syrup on top.

Abby Lincoln died this day,
the radio reports as I make blackberry pie,
the morning after the heat wave broke.
Abby, for whom singing was political, they say…
And who is she? I wonder, the name a haze, Abby,
not Peter, Paul, Mary,
not Janis, Bob or Joan…
and I listen to her wailing notes,
stories issuing forth on iridescent dark wing,
silences uncapped by song and scream.
Sad that her name had not been taught to me,
Her brilliance had not registered with me
until now, her death day…

Only months later do I see her in your photos,
listen to the stories in her words, head toward her truth.

A new pie enters the universe as the radio intervenes again—
the first case of cholera
is codified in Pakistan's not-natural disaster,
and I remember thinking as a child going to India
that cholera must be the worst way to die,
the most dreaded of those diseases
for which we took shots or pills or were forbade to go barefoot—
the largest difference in life for me
a Kansas kid in Orissa.

I remember then that yellow fever shot—
my first trip to Wichita's Air Force base,
on ground which seemed much more foreign
than would the land across oceans
where we were headed.
I wore a leather peace sign necklace to signal
who I was, to that world—
that I was there with contradictory feelings,

the same feelings, I now hold for most everywhere,
knowing now
that there are both macrocosms
and microcosms
that go into Sand Hill Blackberry-Labneh Pie…

Letting them grow as they will: finding prairie synthesis and sustenance duet with my dad

"I don't want to hear about your philosophy unless you can grow corn."
— Winona LaDuke quoting her father,
Vincent LaDuke/ Sun Bear

I.

Man-generated climate change brings us back to the legacy of our land,
part and parcel of something larger and longer:

1000 years ago: Indigenous communities were gardening in Kansas.
400 years ago: Kanzi communities arrived from the east.
Our family lives on what was their migratory, food-gathering land,
just north of what later became the México-US boundary-lines,
and what later still was sold by the US railroad to Mennonite farmers.
With histories of injustices embedded in our land
— in Kansas, like most elsewhere —
we now face climatic shifts that affect everything about how we live.

II.

We will write for people in the future if people now are not interested.
Does that make sense to you?
If there is a future.

III.

Father and daughter drawing on a cornerstone of environmental justice
in Tall-grass prairie-centered ethics and errors,

Drawing on remnants of lessons learned directly through decades of gardening
a plot of loam in league with ecological systems—
native plants and their pollinators—
and, more recently, the deepening wisdom of soil communities.

Drawing on moments of collaboration and exchange, mentorship, research,
rumination, documentation and record-keeping.

Drawing on recognition of our land's peoples,
legacies of injustice that made the land ours to work,
and on measured, but dubious dreams for future climate justice —
we found a poem in our correspondence:

IV.

1940s: After his family moves back to his mother's hometown,
his daughter's hometown-to-be,
he began gardening above Sand Creek,
                             tributary to the Little Arkansas River.

Late 1950s: He comes back to teach,
Returns after three times away— prison (non-registrant), KU (grad school),
Barpali (village Project after Independence)
Orissa, India, — where he & his KU sweetheart married.

Back in Kansas, they garden and preserve food,
his wife gives birth (two times)—
His daughter is born first
she remembers being told they'd ordered orchard trees
from the seed catalog the night before she was born.
She thinks the cherry tree is her twin.

V.

1960s on: He reintroduces native plants to their yard,
not managing it as a prairie garden
nor establishing a full-blown ecosystem,
but letting them grow as they will—
providing space for pollinators, predatory invertebrates,
and others that provide functions to keep a healthy balance.
He gardened organically, but he focused on the garden ecosystem above the soil,
not wondering what the rototiller was doing to the earthworm's home.

V.

Shifting of the Millennium: His daughter shared leaflets about no-till agriculture,
from holistic farm practices that awakened him to the soil ecosystem,
and he decided to try to apply this method to gardening.

His concerns grew for environmental justice with its many dimensions:
There is a lack of justice when our behavior results in damage
to those living in communities more vulnerable to extreme weather or sea level rise.
There is the injustice we are doing to all life on earth,
and there is the injustice to our descendants
who inherit a damaged planet.

Some of these damaging effects come from our food system.
I have been a gardener since I was a youth.
Gardeners work with the soil, not dead dirt, but a living ecosystem.
I have come to realize that some of my gardening practices not only damage
the health of the soil ecosystem but result in the release of extra greenhouse gases
which make our climate more extreme.

As long as I have the energy to garden,
I can experiment with practices to raise my food without these damaging effects.
And so, in a society where competing self-interests rule the day,
I can work on my personal contribution to the common good of environmental justice.
And this gives meaning to life and continues a family legacy of work on justice issues.

III. Westside San Antonio

Mary's gift *(From Meadowlark to Martin Street)*

Upon returning home to sit on my San Anto porch,
I'd rummaged that never-quite-unpacked wicker basket,
pulling out bulbs of last year's garden garlic,
still so sculptural that my neighbors exclaimed
at the Kansas loam, home-grown perfect-ness.

I handed my cross-the-street neighbor
my last jar of your wild blackberry jam "for toast or tortillas"
I noted, tilting jar toward sun
to purple the grayness of the day with deep-color-drenched light:
last summer's sand hills,
morning dew preserved with spirit run wild in that jar—

In a frenzy of post- treatment highs
when you told me the doctor had called you "cancer free,"
you drove out sand roads every day at dawn to find ripe berries,
and at night you'd can the sweet dark fruit
in bell jars, as if your life depended on it.

The morning after my return to San Anto,
my next-door neighbor got tears in her eyes
as we were chatting across the chain link
when our cross-the-street neighbor
came to say their electricity was offed, again
though she'd used grocery money
to pay the (f)utility company the day before.

It had been the cps (f)utility guy chatting loudly on his cell phone
that had brought my next-door neighbor
and me, onto our porches to see the commotion,
and seeing nothing,
we had commenced with our own across-the-chain link chisme
by which time he'd crossed the street, where he ignored our neighbor's pleas:

"My grandchild is with me-- please don't cut the lights."

Conjunto: Dancing for La Gloria I & II

I.

In Kansas there is a Mennonite joke
that says we forbid sex because it might lead to dancing.

And yes, dancing is that basic—
as the First Peoples tell it: Dance is the heartbeat of Nuestra Madre,
red mud trembling, universal frenzy made fuerza unida.

So when I heard they took down La Gloria,
where your grandparents danced their first shy dance,
where El Diablo danced with your prima,
where Tías y Tíos y todas familias came out on summer nights
for rooftop garden parties that rivaled the Menger Hotel's…

When I heard they destroyed the old filling station
with rooftop dancefloor, on April Fool's Day,
seven decades after the building's grand opening,
on Aurelia Elizondo's birthday—
(What better gift could a beloved give…?)
I wondered, "Was that the day Conjunto died?"
Bye, bye, American Pie, y todos…

Sin Conjunto, I fear for the West Side, my neighborhood, now
I fear the devils--not the hoof-footed dancers, but the iron-heeled
who've taken over the radio waves,
replaced Conjunto Tejano del Sur with brand name Spanglish Músicaca—
those devils who turn heartbeats to heartbreaks,
and use nuestra pueblo to build their personal corp-power.

II.

International students foreign to 1950's Kansas
came to Grandma's homestead to dance
away from the college that forbid their traditions.
A decade later, I was growing up there-
--between Bethel, Meadowlark and Sand Prairie—
against the too strict Mennonite order of things
but *with* the blessings of my family's generations.
I remember my grandparents dancing in their den
"move to the music's beat" my mom encouraged,
but grandma let me be off beat.
I wonder, now, how will our generations,
our barrio, continue, if we let them take down our baile,
our Conjunto Dance Gardens?

Where would La Música move upon warm winds,
riding city-night breezes?
Where would music hit down on rooftop
and plazas twirling dancers into tornadoes?
Where would La Calavera Orchestra play?
Where would diablos (y ángeles) dance?
Will Conjunto flee (or rise) to Aztlán?
Will la gente follow their Música?
Will the white egrets, herons & anhinga on Our Lady's Lake
flap sadly to the North Side looking for those who betrayed them?
Will Tonatzín greet the groupies y los grupos when El Conjunto is dead?

Will Rosedale Park, Conjunto Fest Plaza up Martin Street from mi casita,
also fall before bulldozers,
trained in community gardens of South Central LA,
halfway across the continent,
live oaks unearthed like olive trees,
ancient Palestinian groves,
falling to Caterpillars
in yet another occupied neighborhood—
half a world away, yet close enough to feel el grito de silencio,
the aftershock of cultural demolition?

Westside Gardens: No Charge

As darkness lifts—I putter inside and out,
spreading water and good-will,
food for plantas, gatitos y me.
As I walk out the front door,
I see a figure hunched over a plant along the sidewalk—

(I knew when I'd returned a week back
that people, not birds, were eating the piquines this year
because the plants behind the wrought iron fence
still held berries—alizarin swells, even wrinkled ancianas
hung tight—while the bush beside the sidewalk was picked green.)

"Señor, esta planta tiene mas frutas."
I call an invitation, motioning to a branch that drapes over the wrought iron.
The man turns, smiles in warm recognition
of another chili piquín bush, and approaches.
We chat in lengua mezcla as he picks, and I pull dry sunflower stalks:
appreciation for the berries—"buena para salud," "mui rico"
for my yard with plantas diferentes—figs, pomegranate, chaya y nopal
y animales, también—mariposas con muchos colores y abejas...
arañas en las telarañas, gigantic webs...

"En México where I lived, this plant grew everywhere..."
I nod, knowing the landscape from the glisten in his eyes.
"Donde en México?" — "San Luis de Potosi"
We chat in dialect grounded in flora and fauna,
eschewing the monoculture
the city's code compliance imposes.

When he has picked his fill for the day, we exchange names
and he raises his fistful of berries, gently:
"When you want, I will help you here," he says,
gazing at sombra y luz de los verdes... "no charge,"
"No charge," he repeats gesturing to his raised, cupped fist.

                                        August, 2015

Day after Día de Los Muertos at the Rinconcito

A Tiger Swallowtail

wafted over the wall,

over the Tepatate dyed wood shavings

coloring the bare dirt,

and crumbling asphalt,

over the shorn sticker grass

and still struggling strangler daisies—

horse herb blossoms sliced to oblivion,

over the pregnant Ligustrum trees heavy with berries.

The swallowtail passed on to the small yard next door

where a corner-patch of abundant weeds

provides sustenance.

November, 2017

IV. Por La Paz

Questions for Wantin' Times n' Wa-rrr-in' Times and an Answer (Out) of Sorts
Para Juancho—siempre presente por la paz

Why is it you (loudly) self-proclaimed peace people
make me so unpeaceful?

*I am not talking of the Satyagrahi's
or CPTer's, or MECHista's, or C.O.'s or
war resisters or peace marchers
or the weekly vigil-holders in San Anto's zócalo
for the last 10 war years
Nor the peaceable peoples in ashrams, parishes,
hamlets, hoods, barrios, pueblos y colonias
across our world,*

but of the ones who wear Peace as label
compete with corporations & evangelists for converts,
& tell imperfect people like me how to be perfectly peaceful.
I am talking to you
who make me, *the daughter
of 500 year plus–ancient martyrs for peace*, want to go out and draw
a knife around your peace- supremacy world,
put a line in the sand
encircle your space with an inverted wall
where the rest of us don't go.

Why is it me,
who should feel bad
when, finally after decades,
I have la paz en mi corazón (though not in my world)?
Why, when I hear pointedly stable voices despite the hell our world's in…
do *I* feel condemned
reduced to the crime-like the woman,
like the abuser,
alone, but for anger?

Why do I, who abhors shunning,
see my name too, mouthed silently,
as if we are "shhh-cancers?"
Why is it when I—who grew up on prairies and jungles
like a damselfly on the tail of a Kansas breeze—
(no such thing as breeze of course— in their world, KS has only gales…)
why is it I get enraged?

Why do I crumble when I hear you tell of *those* people's children
who have only video war games
no nature, no familia, no calles…
Have you been to the colonias of which you speak?
Do you know whose names
are whispered at nightfall by the people you pity?
Do you know the neighborhood whose stats you quote?

And you Peace People who blast those who came out before you
(*our ancestors, our legacy-bearers*)
for stirring up conflict through their convictions
"provoking" the ones who came after them with chains
and with yellow paint for "yellow bellies"
because they would not buy bonds to war—
Why is it I seethe at your stories?
in ways that rival my responses
to the war-makin' admins & their cronies?

I run away from where the word "peace"
is defamed because I am a coward, stupid, with exasperation,
because I know how badly we have failed,
failed a president who needed his country to give him more than a vote,
to "make [him} do [what was needed for peace]"
failed those made poor or ill by structural Supremacy's violence
failed a planet we disease and dishonor in league with corp-profit,
all the while, denying our complicity.

I am mute because I don't have the words you will hear,
and trembling, because I might have words to rock someone, somewhere.

I run away, and only when stilled in flight, caught in rush hour traffic on I35 glimpse peace as Trojan Horse, caught as well, just ahead of me:

Las Tres Hermanas—Esperanza, Paz y Justicia, Shalom, Shanti, As-Salaam-Alaikum
all echo in my ear as I see the image, read the words
traced with a wet finger in the dust on the tailgate of a semi-trailer
on an inter-continental comet-run,
from Chiapas to Indiana—
stragglers of struggle,
Zapatista face masks carrying peace en sus palabras:

    "Por La Paz."

Eagle Ford Shale: A Free Form Fracking Corrido-Sonnet

Hydraulic Fracturing
Is projectile vomiting—
A violent illness
Poison tinctures en agua,
The liquid forced into the shadows of soils
layered like wedding cakes
of star-crossed unions:
Radioactive. Seismic. Climatic.
Fracking is a
big "forced f'ck" on Earth
in the parlance of us teenage girls in the seventies
coming to terms with what was unspeakable.
Horizontal drilling garners no more
respect for our Madre Tierra.
So take the cigarette ad name
Eagle Ford—a Man, his Truck and his Country--
(Dos Águilas, as they say
at the border
not so far away, when you've gone—down—south)
And Shove It

Shovel It.
Build Loam
Restore Monte
Invite Inmigrantes to return.
Remember La Paz
(Forget the Alamo--
Let it crumble, feed the soil.
Intermingle, with the bones
of the pre-Columbian ancestors of this place)
Let loquat and persimmons grow.
Let los álamos grow back.
Remember La Paz is the Treaty of Two Eagles
Dos Águilas protecting lands and peoples
on ambos sides,
(from each other, and from themselves)
en both lados,
of a river that is confluence more than barrier
like the rivers: San Antonio, Atascosa, Aransas, Frio, Nueces,
and their arroyos…
That the land between these waterways
"is Indian always"
as La Gloria
noted with a pen
that draws, dips in deeper than sword
than plowshare
than drill.

Let the earthworms and microbes
return to this land,
undo the impact of the trucks
and soften the soil, darken it for
all our kin--the gente of
generations going forth
will follow, when we
begin to heal
their lands.

Notes on Envelope: Found Poem from Mt. Zion's Nelson Mandela Tribute,

"For peace, you must forgive"
"Three words for Madiba: Love Peace Unity"

A South African professor, newly arrived at UTSA
says, "In South Africa, there were many students,
like me--in high school in the 80's
in college in the 90s, who were in the struggle,
but unlike me, many of them are not with us anymore.
Many of my generation were killed in the struggle against apartheid."
And we stand to honor his words.

A Methodist pastor says: "In Ghana, a pastor told me:
'You Americans Keep Time. We, Africans Make Time.'"
She says, "In Honoring Mandela I want to say two things:
"There is evil in the world
that must be addressed..."
and she names injustices and isms and violences...
Then she says "There were, and are, women in the struggle...
Winnie was imprisoned too..."
She says, "... anything can change,"
and we stand to honor her words.

And a politician says she was put out of the classroom
for not agreeing with the teacher, and we stand.

And the next speaker says, "There are more Black Men in US prisons today
than were ever enslaved here before...
but as Reverend Copeland said 'I remind you in the spirit of Mandela:
Anything can change.'"
And we stand.

Someone says: "don't just learn about Mandela; learn from Mandela..."
Someone says: "San Antonio has a sister city in South Africa"--

(and I think, I've lived here near 20 years—why didn't I know?)
Someone says, "San Antonio City Council passed a resolution against the Krugerrand"—
(I've heard all the stories, read the histories—why didn't I know?)
And a City Council representative says: "Our children need Mandela's teachings!"
And we stand.

A woman reads Maya Angelou's words:
"In the Alamo, in San Antonio, Texas, on the Golden Gate Bridge in San Francisco, in Chicago's Loop, in New Orleans Mardi Gras, in New York City's Times Square, we watched as the hope of Africa sprang through the prison's doors."
says "Madiba's greatest gift to the world is his 'ability to forgive,'"
says *"we, his inheritors, will open the gates wider for reconciliation, ...will respond generously to [those]...on the floor of our planet."*

And then the oldest Tuskegee Airman takes the pulpit.
He says, on Mandela's 95th birthday, last July,
he'd heard a poem Mandela kept in his prison cell—

The elder started reading *Invictus*, everyday
and so, honoring Madiba, he recited the poem
in Mount Zion, on Sunday afternoon.

*"I thank whatever gods may be
For my unconquerable soul."*

And we stand.

Art is... Manifesto

From first adobe house to embellished stucco repairs I do today, art is companion, process and reprocess, the mediation & meditation of performance & politics, of documentation & composting, of approaches to something indefinable, encased in the crustiness of life, in trial & error, error, error.... In creating curatives, shelter, (en)durability, sustenance, both sublime and subliminal, in traversing the empty breadth and baroque depth of knowledge, art stretches out along novel trajectories & fictions of functionality, reminding me that streams meander for good reason. Great art means re-evolving, producing respect without hierarchy, fondness without bondage, and the wisdom that doing all things right gets her nowhere, which is, after-all, where she will flourish. It means the list of "to do's" never shortens, but neither does it shorten the day's significance with tedium. Art wields the Aryuvedic shield, before, and traipses forth with the steadying balance of a rope bridge beneath, weighing all with the scales of justicia ambiental, of poetic justice and the poetry of the evenhanded. She nurtures maguey, aloe, ruda and romero, waters tulsi daily, and recognizes the timeliness of ambos abortive y fecundity. Art is practicing the origami of alchemy, tincturing shades of sentiment with the purity of oil derived from the incense of deprivation. An artist recognizes she stands and falls on the foundations of politics and poetry built between the chasm of conventionality and the mirage of conviction. She hears one voice and recognizes it as Kali, Tonantzín, Astarte, Atete, as Artemisia, Xochiquetzal, (gendered & un) genius & genus; she hears harmony and recognizes Vishnu, Yahweh and Allah, blessed be, the Great Spirit, por la Paz, Brava..., tierra, agua, todos somos todos, y todos somos dust, todos dust.

# V. Coahuiltecan Land

Borderland Trilogy in Four Stanzas: a Codeswitching Chiasmus, Double Haiku Sandwich & The Bi-National Owls of El Jardín

Palabras Embrace
En Braceros' Palabras

Chichara Summers—
When did drones become killers?
Unmanned means no soul.

According to the men who hold vigil
over the sad wall-building in Hope Park,
there are three white owls
that live in Hotel El Jardín, and fly out predawn
to hunt along the river.
They flap wings slow by the Chisholm Trailhead,
quicken their flight into México each night
and return over the river in the morning
to roost in the abandoned (by people)
garden hotel, to rest in the U.S.

Tejas Afternoon—
Gunfire across the river
Our arms reach their shores.

Kali's Calavera

Kalita gatito
you're no Calavera now--
though after your 11th Canícula
you followed your crazy grito over...,
took mi alma with you to el otro lado.

Rebel rouser to the night you died
and when the next day still dawned
I neglected hell on earth,
and drove you to the crematorium....

Now, like your namesake,
you rein over funeral pyres.
Your tocaya at the mouth of the Ganges
You en la boca del Río Grande y Bravo.

Kalita gatito,
bouncer at the door of heaven
hell cat, love my friends there for me
the way I can't anymore.

Edinburg, 2009

April Litany of Fools' Waivers: An Elegy Found In the Words of the Secretary of "Homeland Security" with Greek Chorus

Said the Archangel Calavera, in 2008,
on April Fool's Day
(You'll remember the date.):
"In order to deter illegal crossings…
there is presently a need
to construct fixed and mobile barriers…
in the vicinity of the border
of the United States."

Said the Archangel Calavera, in 2008,
on April Fool's Day
(You'll remember the date.):
"In order to ensure expeditious construction
of barriers and roads
that Congress prescribed…
in the area of high illegal entry…
I have determined that it is necessary
that I exercise the authority that is vested in me.

Accordingly, I hereby waive
--in their entirety, with respect
to the construction of roads and fixed and mobile barriers
including, but not limited to,
accessing the project area, creating and using staging areas,
the conduct of earthwork,   excavation,
fill,   site preparation,   and installation
upkeep of roads, fences,
supporting elements, safety features, surveillance,
drainage, erosion controls, communication,
and detection equipment of all types:
radar and radio towers,

and lighting [y la luz]
in the Project Area,
all federal, state, or other laws,
regulations and legal requirements of,
deriving from, or related to the subject of,
the following laws, as amended:"

The National Environmental Policy Act
Chorus: HIGH ILLEGAL ENTRY
The Endangered Species Act
Chorus: HIGH ILLEGAL ENTRY
The Federal Water Pollution Control Act
(commonly referred to as the Clean Water Act)
Chorus: HIGH ILLEGAL ENTRY
The National Historic Preservation Act
Chorus: HIGH ILLEGAL ENTRY
The Migratory Bird Treaty Act
Chorus: HIGH ILLEGAL ENTRY
The Clean Air Act
Chorus: HIGH ILLEGAL ENTRY
The Archeological Resources Protection Act
Chorus: HIGH ILLEGAL ENTRY
The Safe Drinking Water Act
Chorus: HIGH ILLEGAL ENTRY
The Noise Control Act
Chorus: HIGH ILLEGAL ENTRY
The Solid Waste Disposal Act,
as amended by the Resource Conservation and Recovery Act
Chorus: HIGH ILLEGAL ENTRY
The Comprehensive Environmental Response,
Compensation, and Liability Act
Chorus: HIGH ILLEGAL ENTRY
The Archaeological and Historic Preservation Act
Chorus: HIGH ILLEGAL ENTRY
The Antiquities Act
Chorus: HIGH ILLEGAL ENTRY
The Historic Sites, Buildings, and Antiquities Act
Chorus: HIGH ILLEGAL ENTRY

The Farmland Protection Policy Act
Chorus: HIGH ILLEGAL ENTRY
The Coastal Zone Management Act
Chorus: HIGH ILLEGAL ENTRY
The Federal Land Policy and Management Act
Chorus: HIGH ILLEGAL ENTRY
The National Wildlife Refuge System Administration Act
Chorus: HIGH ILLEGAL ENTRY
The Fish and Wildlife Act of 1956
Chorus: HIGH ILLEGAL ENTRY
The Fish and Wildlife Coordination Act
Chorus: HIGH ILLEGAL ENTRY
The Administrative Procedure Act
Chorus: HIGH ILLEGAL ENTRY
The Rivers and Harbors Act of 1899
Chorus: HIGH ILLEGAL ENTRY
The Eagle Protection Act
Chorus: HIGH ILLEGAL ENTRY
The Native American Graves Protection and Repatriation Act
Chorus: HIGH ILLEGAL ENTRY
The American Indian Religious Freedom Act
Chorus: HIGH ILLEGAL ENTRY
The Religious Freedom Restoration Act
Chorus: HIGH ILLEGAL ENTRY
The Federal Grant and Cooperative Agreement Act of 1977
Chorus: HIGH ILLEGAL ENTRY
"I reserve the authority to make further waivers from time to time as I may determine to be necessary..."
Said the Archangel Calavera, in 2008.
April Fool's was the date.

Epilogue to the Elegy, for Poetry Month

"Loud and proud/cantaremos/lift our voice
that one collective/ and united/ voz
must not be stilled."
— raúlrsalinas, "Loud and Proud"

    I share this "found" elegy in hopes that we take these words to our communities, our churches and synagogues, temples and mosques, that we take them to our houses and our schools, and to our House of Representatives, to our White House, and to our Courts of Justice. I share this elegy in hopes that we recite it in the places we hold sacred whether in the wilderness or in gatherings of people, whether in the borderlands or the heartland, or on the coasts. All in the USA-- hear this litany of rights and know what we in the borderlands del Valle have lost. And yes, we shall translate it into all the languages spoken in our nation, and in our world— so all understand what has been enforced against communities in the Rio Grande Valley and borderlands, beyond. Before another community's right to clean drinking water is taken away, before another community's right to religious freedom is taken away, Listen! Listen to what was done in our names. Before the right to protect the creatures, the rivers, coasts, harbors, farmlands, even the air... we shall all know what is happening on our one earth, and why.
    The Indigenous in our communities are being asked to sacrifice even that which they hold most sacred, that which we hold dear, that freedom of religion upon which our nation was founded--Are all of you prepared to do the same?
Consider this possibility because we live in a nation that professes
"Equal rights for all," and we live in a world that is ecologically
(if not socio-politically or legally) bound together by the acts we take.
This Elegy is a litany for the Borderlands where high illegal entry upon our rights has been accepted as commonplace; our rights have been waived. As Poetry Month begins in San Anto on the Anniversary of the Fool's Waivers, Poets Recite, Chant, Sing:
High Illegal Entry!

Found Poem: Border Wall Public Comments, Fall, 07
Born into Poetry on the Day of the 67th Nakba in Palestine

The border wall, framed
by proponents as some small regional sacrifice
for a common "security"
offers bogus defense from xenophobic fears--
a security with no credible grounds.

The wisdom & practice of cultura ambiental
suggests such invasive structures diminish the commons
(both cultural and ecological) that come together
in the Texas/ Northeastern Mexican borderlands,
and via migration and immigration,
reach beyond the ends of our continents.

It would be the most mean-spirited *continental* irony
to diminish the commons at the main point of confluence,
but that is precisely what is proposed.

Dichos & research tell us "neighborly" people
keep the safest neighborhoods.
In daily wisdom de la frontera, the truism applies to countries, as well.
Our homeland is secure when we are respectful toward our neighbors,
engendering their understanding of us, their goodwill toward us.
We, borderlanders, fronteristas, protect our commons,
which in turn protects us.

Before cross border shopping, immigrant labor, ecotourism,
before the border itself, we shared ecosystems and cultures—
those original brushlands, river deltas, coastal plains
now altered or destroyed, left behind remnants
that, we on both sides, en ambos lados,
hold in common.

When connected by wildlife corridor
loss of a few acres of habitat on either side,
destroys more than those acres--
the eco-systemic commons is a neighborhood,
a secure, sustaining homeland
as the Kickapoo and their kin know well.

The endangered ocelots' habitat is most famous,
but a border wall's impacts would be a loss to all.
The destruction of a single species is an irreversible loss.

The destruction of the trust we hold with México
in our common natural heritage will take with it
the confianza, shared respect between neighbors
the irreplaceable events of every morning and evening,
in this nexus of migratory routes for birds and butterflies,
in the meeting of tropics and subtropics,
in the merging
of gulf waters, coastal wetlands, and inland brushlands,
in the watersheds of the Río Grande and the Arroyo Colorado
and in the mezcla at Boca Chica Beach
where two countries, one río, and one gulf
converge.

Heed the words of those around the world
separated from family, friends, and neighbors
by the walls of outside forces. For the sake
of all who live in or pass through the borderlands,
from the tiny, rare butterflies
that occasionally leave their Mexican homelands
to grace the Rio Grande Valley with their presence
to the elusive ocelot, to gente with generations on both sides
who cross for quinceañeras, weddings, births and wakes,
and for trekking with abuelos and primas on the monte,
even for the sake of the cross-border shopper (going both ways)--
leave the wall in the box, return it in hopes of a full refunding
of cross-border neighborliness built of the security
that comes of shared wellbeing held in common
with all in our border earth's communities.

Bound

Knowing it might be the last time I'd find calm there,
I'd come to Sabal Palms Sanctuary, before it became "behind the wall"
to find peace: my end of semester chaos
jarred into perspective by a friend's drowning—
his hands tied, his mouth bound, his kind spirit, yet, unbroken.
A Lebanese immigrant dedicated to Palestinian gente—
in recent months, his family had been harassed by FBI/INS/ICE
(that harassment, initiated by misinformation of an informer-solidarity activist,
we later learned-- when by job definition you are lying some of the time
who but God, if s/he exists, knows when?)

The first indication my quest para la paz was doomed
was the flash of white and green metal against the ancient stands of native palms.
When I first glimpsed the couple sitting on the curb at the back of the parking lot
I thought I recognized one young woman—
a student from a past semester?
Our eye met briefly--I'd seen the frenzied weariness of
barely- contained panic, common among students this time of year.
My eyes slid down to not stare into her misery and I glimpsed her hand
bound to her companion's, with a metallic cuff.

Moments later, I sat in subdued conversation with the refuge manager
when the border patrol officer who'd been standing over the couple approached
the refuge office porch. "Do you have water?" the bp asked,
and he was motioned to a fountain inside.
He drank, left, and after a moment, the second officer came for a drink.
My mind flipped back to childhood—
My mother's most basic ground-rule for respect, remembered:
Offer a cup of cooling water.
Compelled to act quickly, I rose,
slid change into the beverage machine, and winced
at the tumble of plastic that set off a brief burst of chatter
among the chachalacas at the feeding station, nearby.
I scooped up the bottles and walked out to the couple.

A wisp of the peace, eluded in my entrance to the sabal monte preserve,
passed overhead gently, as the water bottles passed from my hands
into each of their free ones.
As they grasped the water bottles, in acceptance,
I stuttered, softly, wanting to offer an apology
on behalf of my nation, yet
lacking words in any language.
Still, in the Sanctuary's silence,
the power of our common bond was released,
our common bondage, acknowledged.
Todos somos inmigrantes…

Saturday's Synchronicity II, October 1, 2011

As migratory hawks kettled in the sky over the Río Grande-Bravo
near Anzaldúa's bridge where 1000 youth
planted native seedlings— replanting monte on
once root-plowed wastelands near the banks of the river, behind the new wall
that has divided families and uprooted habitat
like the wall in another long-occupied land across the seas…

As hawks from the north kettled in the Tejas sky, youth
replanted monte beside the new bridge built for semi's, streaming from México,
with goods, allowed to cross where those that make them are not…

As hawks from the north kettled in the Tejas sky,
cops kettled 1000 youth on Brooklyn Bridge—
kettled youth inspired by peers across the seas,
Arab gente in the spring,
themselves inspired by global Satyagrahas
to replace violent power,
    replant democracies' seed,
    plant visions of justice on Wall Street
where banks were salvaged,
and those who make them grow
with their small savings
from scanty earnings,
those who were losing
houses & jobs,
were not saved.

These are Ours

*To you, who gave me the inspiration to write a cussing poem
in cussed times, to those working on the line against the exportation of violence,
and to the students from ambos lados....*

These are ours.
>These are our guns.
>>These are our f'cking guns.
>>>These are our guns firing,
>>>>$s fighting, our gente fleeing
>>>Our taxes train

Our silence feeds
>Our silence feeds upon.

Some silences are imposed by threat of death, but our
silence is chosen for convenience's sake.

Some silences are imposed
>to grow profits,

but our silence is chosen for convenience's sake...

These are our guns.
These are our f'cking
guns. These are our
guns firing. These
are our dollars
fighting. These are
our sons shooting
up... out... at the
breeze,
shooting the breeze...
breezes of wind.

(Wind is soul; Breeze is soulito…
Who shot soul?   Who shot the child of the wind?)

These are our guns.
   These are our f'cking guns.
     These are our guns firing…
       These are our sons shooting

up… out … at the breeze.
These are our sons &
daughters dying.

These are our dead.

Todos somos ….
Todos somos
muertos con grief.

Todos somos
muertos con gritos.
Todos somos gritos ¡Gritos!

Rio Grande/Bravo Watershed, 2018
After Langston Hughes

What do they think
when presidential tweets
threaten El Valle—

The Damsels and Dragons
of Santa Ana?

The Soldiers and Queens on Gregg's Mistflowers
at Mission's National Butterfly Center?

Do nightmares descend upon pollinators
when they hear of the border wall's second coming?
Do Trumpian wars for walls trigger ancestral memories of fleeing
the infiltration of steel and concrete into the borderlands, back in '08?

Do Yucca Giant-Skippers pause on the Spanish Daggers at Boca Chica Beach
to recall tales of canoeists arriving at the small mouth of the grand river,
the eastern end of their trip against a wall along a river, and into the sea?

Do insects wail at the Waivers, rejuvenated from April Fools in 2008?
waivers that spew filth in their air and water
and on the sacred Indigenous vows to protect?

Do the chicharas suddenly shudder? scream? or weep?

Do the mariposas suffer silently?
lose the color on their wings
like mourners?

Maybe they just curl up
and crust over.

Or do they metamorphose?

Emigrantes Ambientales I: After Fallout

Fallout comes in the color of warblers here.
The birds blew in following April chill-storms.
Swallows piling high to stay warm—
some suffocate, as others die
for lack of food—
no insects moving as temperatures glide down.
We will live from crisis to crisis now…

In January, temperatures bottom out,
turn comforter-covered community garden plots
to compost fodder, spoiling new year feasts.
Hypothermic sea turtles, progeny of a hundred million years
are warehoused, bathed in plastic kiddy pools by early responders
hoping to reverse genocide.
We will live from crisis to crisis now…

Drought follows deluge follows drought
The hundred-year drought an annual deal, now.
Time speeds as we age, scientists say—
Is Earth revolving faster?
Can she get away this time?
Eco-empires issue mandates
to catch what the sun has to say,
and at the same time pull poison out
upon the most sacred of pueblos
in order to make core-profit
by lighting the planet
all the while knowing
only nuclear time does not speed up
nuclear does not waste away,
age or reduce to half price.

We live from crisis to crisis now…
What of the next generation?
What of the seventh?

Emigrantes Ambientales II: Valles y Salud

From el valle maravillosa, mágico, delta of the grand river
to Valles San Joaquín and Silicon,
where computer sales sail,
kindles soar above fruit that freezes
or never forms for lack of pollinating bees, or lies unpicked—
where have all the workers gone?
(detention, deportation, disease, fleeing the SB 1070's)—
When will they ever learn? When will *we* ever learn?

No matter, nothing is edible anyhow,
grapes gone "Sun Mad"
as poisons morph proteins in tiny bodies

from Mission to Bhopal
legacies of war from campos en Viet Nam to calles en Chicago
y ciudades from coast to coast.
No juice here, orange, a calavera color, now
its agents reap disease on holy grounds stirring ancient déjà vu
as the continent, herself, recalls the European plagues.

Environmental migrants, illegalized on the corpus of our madre.
felonized in the embrace of our herman@s
país sin tierra,
nations without planet
turtle with no island.
We live from crisis to crisis now…

Emigrantes Ambientales III: Paddling Together

I knew paddling a line down the Rio Grande El Río Bravo
would not be easy though the river carries the canoe
and droplets on wood-grain dry cloudy on the paddle in my lap:
I wince as strangers' border banter pierces my mestiza mind.
Sun and breeze beckon our spirits.
Kingfishers mascot the boats downstream.
Kiskadees and kingbirds call from high branches
against chachalaca chisme,
the gossip issuing from the mesquite and huisache
beyond thickening river cane.
"Two years ago, there were no hyacinth,"
my partner remarks as we steer away
from thick tangles of the succulent green mass,
metastasized—
feeding on the health of its watery host…
We live from crisis to crisis now…

Around a bend in time,
steel and concrete pop up like running bamboo sprouts.
They are leftovers of a far-away war,
warmed over, soldered with the heat of fear—
a border wall to still someone else's demons.
Ours bounce over and back like in an ancient ball game.
We all create crisis, live crises now,
unabated because they stimulate economies and win elections.
Earth and her people, our collateral,
our damaged goods, our sacrificial flesh.
I reach out of the canoe to place a memorial wreathe
on the waters where those who reached el otra lado entered heaven,
while their comrades paced onward
not yet knowing the Estados Unidos might be hell,
knowing only they needed work to pay bills, feed families.
None of us knowing, all earth is in crises together.
None of us knowing, seven generations are in crises together.

Glimpse: a fable for our common future

I

I was there when the rain first arrived.
I was there, as colorless as water-drops before the reflections enter them.
The collision of bodies, clothing and hair was preceded by the collision
of water droplets—
at first, large individual raindrops colliding with drought-drained air,
their weight causing implosions; then, droplets colliding so quickly they morphed
into a stream dissipating what, moments earlier, had been arid, throat-parching heat.

Droplets would rise in a slow bounce of steam from the crusty earth.
They would beam on people's faces like the sweat of passion.
They would ting the concrete and steel of the wall releasing an acrid smell,
unlike that sweet, wild pungency the first rains had gifted countless generations
on both sides for millennia. The smell did not damp down the miracle, though
some say it was an omen in the end. A glimpse of recognition followed the
collision of bodies, passing from one pair of eyes to the next. A common glance—
the fusion of terror, compassion, empathy and dread— a collusion of souls.
How did each person recognize that the patterns coming in mirrored those
passing out of them? — that I may never learn, but I saw it happen.
People stared into the midst of the chaos and saw their own ambivalence echoed
in the eyes of dreaded strangers—and they bonded.

Perhaps it was because the rain did not arrive powered by thunder
or on wings of lightning.
Perhaps the collision of bodies and subsequent mixing of souls released
the storm's energy through humans, this once—
a sidestepping of the usual passage through the elements.
Perhaps it was the release of pent-up rage stifled by futility of bare survival
and swelling with heat that preceded rain?
Or was it the recapture of gases passing through holes rent in the skies?
Or the gathering of gases—churning un-tethered, seeping from the chronic,
corporate power burning at earth's heart?

Later, I hear, these possibilities would all be debated and theories about them
delivered and debunked, but at the time no one questioned the wisdom passing
through the dance of raindrops and bodies. If they saw cause and effect at all,
they believed that with the miracle of rain came cleansing:
a complete healing of earth was taking place,
and oppressive powers, once so prevalent,
were dispersed to dust, which ran clean in the rain.
It was as if all the grief that rolls away on tears never existed.
This, people believed, without question, at the time.
I was there when, like chameleons, the rain-drenched bodies began to radiate
in reflections and burst open in color like the northern skies in aurora borealis,
like reptiles in mate.
It was as if Kodachrome caught the full measure of life
from each of us and distilled it into that momentary, colored ocean.

II

I was there for the melting of the wall that some said had caused the drought.
That wall had caused death—
not just humans passing through purgatories to get around it—
but other animals too—from the hummingbird to the eagle, butterflies
and the cats who stayed in the wild
when their compatriots took up residence by the fires of woman.

Melting may not be the proper term to describe what happened—
no one felt heat, but the wall did not crumble, fall or explode.
Rain-drenched, the wall simply began to run,
and like a long shroud of cloth, that was not colorfast—
it unwrapped in brilliant tributaries chased by rain torrents.
In the end, it joined the river like an ephemeral stream.
Some say it lurks still with shipwrecks' lost treasure on un-swept ocean floors.
With the passing of the wall, the next stage of miracle emerged.
On what had been each side, people saw anew what lay next door.
Elders recognized the sight of the neighboring land,
for they had been young when the wall was built.
They called out the names of landmarks—
 buildings, parks and even the sacred names of mountains
that had been hidden by the wall.
But for the younger ones the sights were new
for after the wall's erection, cross- border visits had ceased.

Families reunited and kin who were strangers were introduced.
The long-lost found how close they'd been all along.
For animals, though, an instinct—no longer intact in most humans,
an archive of collective experience—
led them immediately to places they'd never seen in their lifetimes.

All mourned anew the groves of trees, wilderness and gardens taken out by the wall.
In lost flora were thousands--maybe worldwide—millions
of cumulative years of growth, of time spent sustaining the rest
from the tiniest of organisms to the largest of animals.
They mourned the plants' ritual—
the daily cleansing of the elements in earth and sky.
When the elders remembered the trees, they remembered teachings:
"Plant these trees for your grandchildren, not for yourselves."
They glimpsed the earth,
despairing at first for no seed
had been saved.

III

Some say, yet another miracle—
seeds had gone nowhere,
and with the washing away of the concrete,
the gentle embrace of soil and the wet arousal of rain,
they split open and shot green toward sky.
Some came out quickly, some more slowly,
but the green life of the land was returning.
Leaves shot up like surprise lilies after thunderstorms.

Children scampered about finding new patches of growth in unexpected places.
They called elders to come identify what kinds of plants were beginning life anew
at each spot. Sunrays came then to nourish the green
and with the sunlight, the rain joined the sky again and I, on its back...
can tell no more,
can only describe when the rain arrived.
I was there, as colorless as water-drops before the reflections enter them.

 From there on out, this story is yours.

VI. Payaya People's Home

City of Tiny Terrors

Today this city is a poem of tiny terrors.
They say this city is a poem of wonder,
though magnetisms have been switched out,
One force for the other.
What once comforted, rebels.
What once crooned, grumbles.
What once welcomed, repels.
What once sustained, crumbles.

Memories have lost their cohesions.
Bridges have gone behind walls
that separate generations and terminate symbiosis.

I want to plant spring seeds,
but time has run askew, drained away—
The sun has not returned, has been deported.
Each morning, I wake in anticipation
but sense as I rise, the weather is not right.
So instead, I pour water in a clay saucer. I feed cats.

You say you do not know trust, anymore.
Neighbors have been detained, deported with the sun.
You do not know neighbors.
There are no neighbors.
There is no one left whom you know.
Neighbors have been evicted.
They have nowhere, now.
Their puppies sit in a wire cage, awaiting fate.
It doesn't come. We pour water in a tin bowl. We feed dogs.

I read the news, like all of you:
San Antonio is a model for the world:
A wonder of globe-washing, new, clean Tri-centennial city.
A Guardian of Goodwill on the Planet.
I scoff: For their world, perhaps,

but not our neighborhood.
For their planet, perhaps
but not for people like us,
    not for the animals,
        not in our times of tiny terrors.

Resistance Plantings at Hay's Street Bridge People's Park

The People's Park beneath Hays Street Bridge
was an unoccupied wasteland lot,
when I went out to scatter seed of hairy vetch.
I dropped black, BB-sized seeds
into crusty dirt mounds amongst
tufts of straw-hued grass blades
while thinking how the chains of lacy-leafed legume
ending in purple petals would feed and fortify the city soil.

One time, my neighbor helped me broadcast seed,
and after we finished off the repurposed baggie of seed
and looked in vain for evidence of earlier plantings,
we returned to a truck that refused to start.

(I should have known not to drive my pick-up there
where the city backs men who want
to take away the dreamed-of park—
for my pick-up stalls at places where mean spirits are at play--
witness her frequent stalls at border patrol checkpoints.)

I never saw that any of our vetch took root—
there was mud for a short while after days of deluge,
then the top crust was bull-dozed away
making an impervious surface.

I expect though,
there is still some seed in that soil waiting
for the People's Park
to take root.

p.s. One of my "resistance plantings" did take root as
a vine at the base of the border wall being built
at Brownsville's Hope Park…
I imagined border-crossers
taking heed of the green twining up the steel wall
might smile, for a moment.

HDRC TESTIMONY

I agree that this building diminishes viewshed
and greenspace, for Hays Street bridge communities
                         and those who visit her.
                  And I would add another dimension
         to the stance that the building does not meet standards
                            for quality lifeways in our city.
                     I ask for holistic justice, that is—
                that we look into the combined effect,
         the combined impact of this project on particular place
                                and broader
                                 implications
                                  on our city.
                    On the eastside border of downtown
                   where homes meet Railroad and Bridge
              We need space for the ground to breathe,
                            to soak in falling rain
                                This place matters.
                   Hays Street Bridge communities matter.
                 Don't risk implosion of dense matter
                        the focus on money's hosting
        that ignores the structure of violence it thrives on.
             The eco that forgoes ecology for economy only
                    The free trade that forgoes fairness
   forgets that children need rain-drenched flowers to play in
                 elders need places to walk gently.
              We all need air that feeds our lungs.
                       What we do here matters.
                       What the CoSA does,
                    What you do, matters.
                Density is not infinite, and it is not
                an automatic environmental win.
                     Listen to the empty space
                   Listen and look to the air
                   Hear the aesthetic space:
                  Need space for spirits to dance
             on the eastside border of downtown.

Your decisions need to take these aspects into consideration
to consider holistic justice. Hole with the "w" from the world....
Bridge against blue hole that is sky, red sphere that is sun,
white sphere of moon.
Air that we can see across.
A place where we can see each other wave.

What Gravity Reveals

I.
When it all became too much, I stopped fighting gravity—
if something falls and there's no pragmatic reason for it not to
be on the ground, I don't pick it up. Making conscious decisions
about whether to engage with minutia helps me clarify and
organize priority thoughts and actions.
The horrific absurdities, ironies and crises stand out;
the mundane, personal slights fall to the wayside as mere creative clutter.

II.
"All this cutting and scraping and hoping and praying,
all this pain is
going to be for naught if the insurance won't pay
for the hospital's oxygen treatments."

"But your new doctor, the surgeon you met when he recognized your wife
as his patient assistant for years--he did your latest surgery; he won't let that
happen. He's the one who happened by on New Year's Eve when you were
back in the emergency room after two weeks' of increasingly excruciating
pain, following the last cut toe—your new doctor will care. He cares about
you, and about his work coming undone if you don't get the treatments."

"But he's done his job. It is out of his hands. Now the decision on the oxygen
tank lies with the Insurance Co., with Medicare and if they deny me…"

"Well, if they don't authorize the treatments, can you say you'll bring in a lawyer?
I can look for someone."

"By then it will be too late."

His wife gets on the phone, then, and says assuredly: "No worries now.
We are in the hospital for the weekend--nothing will happen until Monday."
We laugh grimly.

III.

Soon after moving to San Antonio, I was shuffling bookshelves around my office on a Sunday afternoon and pinched my thumb. Worse than the throbbing was my panicked realization that I had no idea where in this town I'd go for medical care. Nearly 20 years later, I still don't know. My work now brings in little financial compensation, not enough for me to have any insurance access given I'm not old enough for Medicare and living in a state that didn't expand Medicaid. So, a few years back I dusted off an old college textbook from a course in rural development: *Where There Is No Doctor*; later, I supplemented the worn but rugged hardcopy with a free copy I found online. I prefer them to the medical websites that so often—like most of society, these days— have ulterior monetary profit motives when offering advice. While I live in a neighborhood down the street from renowned hospitals, one with a tiled angel mosaiced on its high walls, another illuminating the night with revolving-color lights, I live in a neighborhood that exists in the shadows of those metropolitan health care systems. I am grateful that my parents have healthcare access, even if the nurses in their small town are forced to work shifts that would be illegally long if they were truck drivers. I am as worried for those nurses as for my family. I am grateful that I have no children for whom I could not afford a doctor; I barely managed emergency vet bills when my cat got an abscess that would not go away, this fall.

IV

Growing up in Kansas, my great uncle was my doctor. Once he tickled me so hard that when, afterward, he took my blood pressure, I had laughed so much, it was high. We had to go back the next day, and it tested normal. I felt apprehension, then, because, unlike in school, I didn't feel like I had control of how well I did in the doctor's office. The doctors during our family's sabbatical—my dad teaching in Orissa (now Odisha), India, were often my parents' previous co-workers— family friends. During a college class in Guatemala, we met with doctors practicing in small, crowded cement casitas on pastoral hillsides, doctors who were part of the communities they served, not unlike my family's doctors, growing up. Since then, doctors have often felt out of reach for me.

V

My dad just called. I haven't told you that my mom is in the hospital for a bout of atrial fibrillation this week. My concerns for her health are behind my current preoccupation with the odd logic of our medical facilities. When she was in critical care, there was a high nurse to patient ratio. My mom was in pretty good spirits on a floor with very ill patients. The nurses talked and laughed with her; they took my mom for a walk and wheeled her down to their station rather than leaving her alone while preparing her new room. Outside critical care, my dad said there were fewer nurses with more patients and less healing, down-time to spend. I mentioned my friend's worry about his Medicare Insurance not granting time in the hospital for continuing the oxygen treatment his legs needed. My dad reminded me he'd had to sign a paper the first day as my mom was admitted stating that they'd been told they could appeal if Medicare was requiring the hospital to dismiss her before they thought it was advisable.

"Oh, thank you, that's it then, I'll let my friends know they can appeal to stay for the oxygen treatments the doctors are recommending." I replied, happily.

VI

As I prepare to call my friends, I am thinking about the near fifty years of changes in medicine since my childhood, about medicine here, and in far-away places, about the enormous increases in medical technology and bureaucracy. All that falls away though, as I realize that the connections that count, the basis of healing, medicine's community, these remain intact despite the profit-driven clutter, through friends, among family.
Gravity prevails, like love gone cold.

Epistle del Amor

"How can one marry... but to some portion of the earth?"

Cuidad de San António, Mi Corazon,

Your Blue Hole is centering the universe even as the planet wobbles
in feverish winds and trembling firmament. Yet in San Anto, we go about
our complacent, sometimes happy lives. Is it because we have survived
so much in the devastating formation and expansion of our city?

San Anto del Sol, del Solar ...I love how the sun transforms the color of you,
multiplying greens in spring, drying earth crisp browns in summer. Floods
sweeping off of impervious cover in October, where your caverns that
once held excess, have been cemented in, and water tables have dropped,
irreparably. Yanaguana, ancient place of waters that refresh us, San Pedro
Park, compatriot of Boston Commons-- Springs, now dried like old age dries
our bodies in preparation for our return to dust.

San Quilmas, I love that we hold together never letting loose of our
heartstrings, in jail or out. Mi Esperanza, Nuestra Fuerza Unida, I love that
La Lucha continua, that even when parched by hot sun on dry earth or frigid
winters that chill air and then bones, we keep a constant beat...
en las calles y en los corazones.

San Antonio, I love you for holding onto earth's sacraments.
Even as land herself is torn asunder by economy-boosting escapades,
your Blue Hole maintains our sacred balance.

    Hold me, Yanaguana, until you return,

VII. Maternal Inheritance in Times of Great, Great Hate

Contemplating Complexity

"You cannot be at home with something that you feel is wrong...."
— Representative John Lewis, 1-13-17

I. On Call
What does it mean to be "at home"?
What does it mean to be "on call?"
These days (and nights) I teach courses online.
I am "at home" most of the time, but on-call "24-7."
Some days, time collapses, and every happening of my day —
deadlines, dedication, dishonoring, delirium, disaster—
mishmashes together in asynchronous mush.
Is this like a doctor's life?
I wonder if doctors and teachers have a lot in common.
I wonder, where we can be "at home,"
now that both groups seem under redefinition along with the ACA, the EPA,
and another zillion acronyms for the small progress of decades
that is under assault?
Is even this alphabet itself at risk
in what is now casually called a post-truth world?

For survival's sake, old age prepares me with wry wit,
a stability necessary for this kind of teaching--
the technology didn't exist when I was younger,
nor did my solidity.
Yet, for the first time in many years,
I am less sure about the permanence of our town,
its ability to survive, even less, our nation's capacity to sustain.
I am dubious about survival, overall, in our planet's feverish future:
I was a child of "Silent Springs," first Earth Days, and my country's endless war.
I came of age marching in the nuclear freeze movement.
For awhile, after that, more walls were crumbling than being built.
And after decades of back & forth,
I saw a president who had joined the cries from the margins:
"Yes, we can." "Si, Se Puede."
And we did, at least on some matters.
Now, like millions, I am answering calls, nonstop,
but I can't find my way *home*, in my nation.

II. Phenology and Ornithology
I learned to listen attentively by listening to birds in the prairie,
and later the jungle. I learned to distinguish characteristics of species—
birds, herps, wildflowers through close observation and magnification.
I picked up on shades, tones and hues, textures, and rhythm.
I was taught to record the times when plants bloomed and went to seed.
I learned to put these things together into stories and to test their truths.

III. Close Reading
College gave me new names for collective connections,
and in grad school, I learned the intense intimacies
of old-fashioned, literary "close readings"—
through Third World Feminisms.
Close reading, the purview of "New Critics,"
was used in our hands to delineate the world with the "aha" and awe for
equity, showing the social structures the New Critics vacuumed away—
in this case, we found the master's toolshed, useful.

IV. Canicular Connection
The day my mom turned 65, my dad planned a series of surprises for her.
On her birthday, my brother and I arrived in our heartland hometown,
unanticipated.
My mom screamed her delight so loud the cross-the-street neighbors could hear.
Our family jumped in the car then, to make the Indian lunch buffet, 25 miles away.
After stuffing ourselves as we do only with curries, we went walking around
the zoo. Suddenly my mom felt light-headed and had to sit down. Being
outside in mid-August dogdays hardly seemed the problem:
my mom had spent more than three score of summers in the heat, without AC—
playing, studying, giving birth... (my brother's birthday was coming up in two
days...) cooking, canning, cleaning, cultivating good living in the plains of India
and the US, always busy, even on the hottest of Canicular Days.
After resting in the shade, she felt fine, and we continued to celebrate.

V. Contemplating
Around that time, stability took leave of my mother's blood pressure—
"We can medicate to bring the spikes, down, and the falls, up."
we were told— "nothing moderates, though."

Yet, I'd learned from mom, early on, to negotiate life's ups and downs—
turn into the curves, go with the flows, and bring things back around to balance—
if I danced right, the weight of the world would be at rest above my solar plexus.
Can our bodies not continue to do likewise into old age?
Or is instinct kicking in at the wrong moments disrupting
what elements of ourselves have never made adjustment to modern life?
Looking back, I wonder, if mom's decade of dementia
has been a consequence of the high or the low, the leap between the two,
or likely, all three.
It may be only a correlation.
Or, perhaps, none of the above.
The fact is, we are still far from knowing truth.

VI. Complexity of Connection
That "knowing" is difficult, I have no doubt.
Still, I cannot imagine its impossibility.
My mom, into her mid 80's now, takes blood pressure regimens
based on the BP readings my dad takes from her several times each day.
For years, she has gone into ER for what they write down as "orthostatic
hypotension." The medical personnel are not around when her BP plunges,
but when they see her, they assume it happened when she stood up,
suddenly, because that is what's common.
Truth is, her blood pressure wasn't dropping when she stood up.
No, it was often after a meal—like the time at the zoo after her birthday feast.
For a while, in the back of my mind I wondered if it was some combination
of spices. Then I read something online about "postprandial hypotension"—
blood pressure that bottoms out after a meal, the more food, the deeper the plunge.
I applied my close reading skills and my ecologist's strengths of observation:
it wasn't the heat or spices—it was the amount she'd eaten.
By the time I'd thought this through,
it was not just large meals that impacted my mom's blood pressure—
after breakfast, it was especially likely to register low making her feel groggy.
When I saw how the similarity in my mom's symptoms after meals and the
definition matched up, I sent the words "Postprandial Hypotension" on to my dad,
who mentioned it to their doctor who changed prescriptions so a pill before a meal
could help counter the dip before it happened.
A few less disasters in the mishmash.

VII. Teacher's Resolve
As we begin the new year, I ask students to write their stories—
knowing their words will help us recall,
remind someone of what it used to be,
to be "at home."
Someday, someone will make the connections.
Undo the wrongs.
Someday, we will lay down the wry wit,
and feel at home with small, progress, again.

Epistle, Friday, January 13th, 2017

Mom,
One night, three decades back,
you told me you'd nightmared:
Wordsworth, your small press co.
was in danger,
and you, trying to save it,
passed it on
to me, your daughter—
as an inheritance
of work and words to protect.

And three decades later
as we glance away from tyranny
taking hold of our lives,
a word's worth is endangered by fake claims.
I am teaching again, online this time--
some students' words would nail my name
onto some post-truth, "professor watchlist"
though my pedagogies,
the soil under my fingernails,
the letters my hands hold
and the stories I type
are composed
of decades formed
of mulch & marches.

Mother, I want to put your stories
down in word—
an antidote to this malevolence.

I want to write the stories down
so you can read and reminisce.
I want to write the stories you'd told us family,
write what you'd never put to paper

for you wrote down other's stories,
published others' stories
before your own
held your life back from print,
yet lived the march
behind your words.

For My Mother,

In the six weeks
between Christmas
and my birthday
as goodwill waned further in our world
and your mind, body and soul
finally drifted apart from us,
I desperately wanted milagros…
but as you had guided us to see,
there is history and hard work
behind miracles.

I had wanted to repeat your memories
so, even in dementia, you might recall,
how you laughed with your brothers—
chattering children in Kansas,
growing up in a world at war,
migrating from town to town
for your parents' teaching jobs.

Now I tell others—
how you lived larger,
made more with less, than we do now,
made do, without regret,
lived for a while in a bank building…

In 2006, driving north from Newton
we stopped in Glendale
found those brick bank walls
standing, open air now,
the bones of the building, foundation
complete enough for you to recall
where your mother cooked
and where your family ate, where you slept…

We drove up past Minneapolis, Kansas
to a border-with-Nebraska town
to pick up a pick-up, a 1995 Nissan
I purchased with some meager funds you'd saved
for me to follow a teaching job
just north of the border our country
drew with Mexico, over a century back,
and is re-drawing every day, in blood
and now in cement & steel,
and now in words devoid of truth.

So much that is happening is an affront to how you lived:

You wrote down the good of others' lives,
and lived the work behind your words.
You were not judgmental,
but had old-fashioned words that nailed obscenities that wound.
Often, in recent months when I've heard the latest news-tweet:
Filthy, Vulgar, Obscene, Livid—my outrage comes out in your words, Mom.
Though you condemned wrongs,
it was actions, not people you considered bad.
There were no bad people in your world.

At end of your large life,
you passed on alongside many other elders
shifting burdens,
transitioning without full cognizance of the hate
increasingly festering about our world.

You all made beauty, art, love,
burgeoning milagros out of your lives.
We now must scrub through the "filth"
to find the foundations you left shining.

Postscript: February, 2017

Mom,
In a sense
our relationship is one long Mobius strip—
a twist upon a smooth path
with no boundaries—
an end that leads to a beginning.

The day our nation distilled the doom
of decades, upon decades into a single figure,
I made a Haiku placard that read:

"World Citizens
Planetary Patriots
Hijas del Mundo"

The next day, and many days since,
I held that sign, high—For Us.

We talked maybe once
after that. Then, when I called
and dad put the phone on speaker
for you both,
you only listened.
But I know you knew
Mother, that I carried that sign for you:

Daughters of prairie and village
Daughters of Madre Tierra.
World Citizens
Planetary Patriots
Hijas del Mundo

La Despedida/The Sendoff, May 27, 2018

Dear Mother,

We have gathered on Memorial Day weekend,
here outside the church you joined 60 years ago.

I remember in childhood,
hearing you explain that we didn't so much celebrate
Memorial Day with parades, as others might,
but we would remember our relatives with stories
and commemorate those who lived & died
for peace, for justice, for all.
This letter is for you and to you, on both counts.

Mother, it is good that your
ashes are to be scattered here—
you are the first from this church,
from this community
to join the millennia of living beings,
whose remains lie
in these soils: Kansas, prairie—once seabed—soils.

We are of this place, of this earth,
composed of soil's decomposition
and re-composition.
We remain a part of these fertile soils.
We remain to feed this place.

From childhood, I remember Bible verses
about coming from and returning to dust—
From teen years, I recall from the *Kansas* song:
"*All we are is dust in the wind*"
and it seems so appropriate, here,
though your skepticism taunts me—
the irony of these poetics was not lost on us.

Dust was something to get rid of with a rag & lemon oil
usually on Saturday morning.
You deemed dusting, a desirable job—
we got to touch the Bharati carvings of egrets and elephants,
the photos of relatives & friends, abstract wood tones,
and many treasured books.
Dust was in the wrong place. People were not…
or if they were, they could move. People could be moved
and they could be moved to *not be moved.*

Dust and hay fever were forever your nemesis
bringing on itchy eyes and runny nose—
Maybe this too, was why you didn't welcome
a return to dust…

I remember discussing
the difference between dust and good garden dirt
around the dinner table
in a kitchen where we did battle with both.
In the early years we didn't realize
the extent to which soil is living
(Well, both dust and dirt, actually, are alive—
dust with mites to make you and I sneeze,
and soil with microbes to grow
the fruits, veggies and flowers of our labor.)

Dust is to dirt or soil
what weeds are to wildflowers or native grasses…
And you were one to see the nuances, to see something anew,
and if you became convinced, you joined in.

And I quote your words now:
Then I saw a patch of prairie grass without the frame.
And there it was <u>exactly</u> like it had been in the woodcuts—
repetition of line with variety of color.
(Even that same shade of pink that I had wondered why [the artist] used
because it didn't seem like what I thought of as a prairie color.)…

*As striking as any new perspective I've ever encountered through words,
I saw the prairie in a new way, linked to the art prints I had seen the day before.
I think I drove faster, my eyes flashing ahead to see how the next patch of pasture
looked by itself with the variations of light—no longer framing it with fence posts
or hedge rows or horizons, not even needing a taller grass or a plant of a different
shape to border the composition. The world seemed bigger, while at the same time
I felt more a part of it and it was more my own, than it had been the day before.*

Mother, it is good
that we scatter your ashes here
in this soil that is returning to prairie,
lifting our spirits as we remember
the lessons you shared
when you first saw your friend's abstract art
of prairie grasses.

You were good with transitions in perspective,
toward better ways of seeing, of being,
toward growing-- flowers and goodwill,
justice, peace and freedom.
You worked *"From the Idea to the Printed Page."*
as your Wordsworth business cards read.
And now, the full extent of your cells remains in ashes
and those ashes will become one with the soil,
with the grasses, with the wildflowers, with the wind.

Mother, I remember you singing with your autoharp—
songs from Joan Baez' songbook:

"Where have all the flowers gone? Long time passing"--
Pete Seeger's composition from a Russian folksong against war
with Hickerson's verses that made it a circular song:
"Where have all the flowers gone? Long time ago."
Flowers, to girls, to young men, to soldiers, to graveyards, to flowers…

*"Where have all the graveyards gone?
gone to flowers, everyone."*

When the bougainvillea was in full bloom at my place in San Antonio,
my neighbor, x-daughter-in-law to the family that built the house
and planted the bougainvillea, said to me she wished to take a bouquet
of bougainvillea to her mother-in-law. I was glad to give her the flowers,
though I knew her mother-in-law had died
some years before I bought the house.
Only later did I fully comprehend—
the bouquet of bougainvillea was going
to her mother-in-law's grave in the San Fernando Cemetery.

In this Peace Garden, ashes will feed ancient soils
that will nurture the flowers
that will honor the souls of those whose ashes are scattered here.
We commemorate their lives and spirits
as well as those who remain here from across the millennia,
those who visit, those blown in by wind.
We see in the prairie grasses
that *"the world seem[s] bigger,*
while at the same time
[we feel] more a part of it
and it [is] more [our] own…"

With my love,
Kamala

VIII. Westside Atzlan

Ardeidae Anthem
We shall not, we shall not be moved.

I am Bird Island
Place of White Herons
Aztlan

I am earth formed of
cast off remnants of well-lived lives--
crumbling stone & crushed bone--
decomposed before Our Lady's lake waters
engulfed my soils to form shores.

I am Bird Island
Place of Great Egrets, Anhinga
Aztlan

Semillas sprouted in my soils.
Fleshy petals topped forbs with color,
slender-leafed sedges and rushes greened,
pulsing organs gave birth to fauna:
Pollen-fed insects on wildflowers graced my floor.
Small birds & fruit-eaters in understory
and Ardeidae Family birds began to roost
in branches of cypress, huisache, willow, mesquite.

I am Bird Island
Place of Many Egrets
Aztlan

Peoples passed through these rich lands,
gathered near arroyos and now-parched springs
that sustained the waterways that surround me.
Later people bought and sold the Coulson Tract,
Elmendorf Lake grew, fed by streams.
Neighborhoods formed: Lake View, Westend, Prospect Hill—
people joined the cyclical comings and goings
at the park. They named me after the birds.

I am Bird Island
Place of Cormorants Egrets and Herons
Aztlan

Great Egrets were always here, as were Snowy,
Cattle Egrets came later, journeyed from Africa.
Decades passed, secrets disclosed, now forgotten.

Police took their breaks on my shores
gathered to drink beers donated by
once prolific mom & pop tienditas.

Nationwide, the Great Egrets barely survived the feather-mongers.
After their comeback, though, they became an emblem of revival—
Audubon's mascot.

Egrets dance and prance for each other,
bring offerings of sticks for nest-building. At night
they trill lullabies that fade into guttural, soothing sleep sounds.

But the sanitizers came over
to sweep clean the neighborhood—
the joggers, the house flippers
the "gente-ficators" who
disliked the egrets, disdained the broken hearted,
decided to displace the generations of people and birds.

"Send them to Mitchell Lake," someone said.
The Idea was born on the wake of canons and pyrotechnics—
strategies to dismantle my existence are in place, are being
carried out in a powerful assault.

Yet I am still Bird Island
Place of Ardeidae
Birds of Aztlan

Egrets' Elegies
After Derek Walcott

I. Winter of Westside Displacement

First days of December,
city workers don white hazmat suits,
prefiguring the prevalence
of pandemic protective garb.
Men board motorboats and rafts, journey out,
and with the slow, deliberate fury
of a 21st Century cyclone, they make landfall,
deboard into an Advent Season Pantomime
inspired by Avian phobias.
By the beginning of Halcyon Days,
they have denuded Bird Island.

Following USDA "Wildlife Service" edict
the men in suits remove all nests.
Audubon volunteers
transfer six nests south of town,
rewire them into trees
on the banks of recycled sewage waters
where other waterfowl abound
and people visit from the northside.

Around this time, on the other side of the earth,
a random, novel corona virus, animal borne,
took up residence in a human.
As people sicken in Wuhan,
pyro-techniques, lasers, drones, scarecrows,
and noise warfare are used to terrorize
the Ardeidae Family homes on Bird Island.

Of the 56 fledglings, taken from nests
and under Wildlife Rescue's wing,
15 cormorants are still living by end of January.
By then, unbeknownst,
Covid 19 is spreading in the US.

Egrets who had not already migrated down the Gulf,
some who fledged last Spring,
roost on small trees along the shoreline
behind the now desolate island
from which the Ardeidae Family has been displaced.
A few cormorants remain on the ground,
contemplate rebuilding on barren soil.

Across the Westside barrio, displacement threatens
Alazán-Apache, Los Courts, built, 1937.
Generations of birds and people who share decades, neighborhoods,
la paz en el barrio, to be sent packing.

One sunny afternoon, two Great Egrets
venture out on the island's barren ground:
they arch wings and dance,
rising in rhythm
each with the other
dancing to drumbeats
we cannot hear.

Perhaps they know that science
now says mating seasons are becoming erratic,
cycles disrupted by climate chaos.

Do they sense that when the
pandemic-spreading-in-the-community
closes all schools, churches and "non-essential business"
they, along with other egrets and a squad of Little Blue Herons
will be harassed, and for a second time, displaced
from the trees they have chosen for roosting
at the edge of the Blue Star by the San Antonio River?

Do they fear the spirit of distancing
will prevail across the avian world, as well?
Do they fear the illness, itself?

One sunny December afternoon,
two Great Egrets
venture out
on the island's barren ground.

Their dance defies the city
that denies them roost and nest.

They dance a final dance, fly off,
follow waters to the Gulf.

II. Essential Business

Sunset brings out harassers—
youth toting pyro-technique handguns battle the egrets,
propane canons arch and flame above the island,
over the roadway, grazing sacred limestone spires that once caught fire.
Human neighbors droop as they walk, distraught at the antics
intensifying in the advancing Advent season.
By Solstice, up to 100 Great and Snowy egrets air-dance—
They cluster in spontaneous troupes,
circle-cross the Westside skies.
Each night when their harassers leave the park, they swoop in
settling on the bank's saplings near the nursery side
of the island where they were raised.
But by January, they do not return to land in late evening.
A phone text photo reveals they found a backyard tree near Woodlawn Lake.
They will not be moved far from their barrio.

Cattle Egrets were the professed target of early assaults.
In late winter, as Corona's Catrina Calavera arrives in the US,
around the year one anniversary
of the public release of egret displacement plans
Parks has expanded their plans--
they now will disperse all migratory birds from Bird Island.

Backyard Bird Count, a week later,
Snowy, Great and Cattle egrets in ones or twos
approach the island where a dozen cormorants gather at the shoreline.
Ardeidae Family fly up to perch on Bird Island's Blue Willow cypress,
still void of the spring blooms that hang heavy
with promise on other cypress in the park.
The birds' rhythm, their curves of synchronicity chant:
We shall not, we shall not be moved.

March begins balmy all along the Gulf
as more migratory egrets and herons come inland.
The disease, now proclaimed pandemic, overspills hospitals,
and soon after, mortuaries, and obituary columns, around the world.
Parks Dept. declares war on all migratory birds in the City of San Antonio.

April brings big chills and searing heat to man and beast,
tornadic winds blow chaotic with the Planet's rising fever.
Up North, out west and in the Southeast, Cancer Alley LA,
elders with hearts and lungs damaged by decades
of incinerator-dirty air in neighborhoods of color
breathe faltering breaths, alone,
in the metal arms of a ventilator if one is available.
People interaction is now online, digitized to protect some of us.

When egret breeding brings out filigree feathers that wisp across one's wing
when buff colors appear on Cattle Egret backs, bringing couples together,
the Ardeidae Family's displacement becomes "essential business"
along with the Bexar County jail, packed with those who cannot pay bail,
along with ICE adding detainees to their illness-invested coffers,
along with rental agencies defying Texas eviction moratorium
to lock people out of their homes—their safe place (or is it?),
along with police, faces uncovered, brutalizing the bronze
bodies of Westside neighbors.

From Gulf to Gulf, planetary oil has glutted.
The filthy flow that pipeline protests
and protection camps on Indigenous land
had only slowed, a pandemic has halted.
In Texas, the toxic stench that decades of coastal communities fought,
as they lived daily through flares of sour crude, flare ups of chronic disease—
Black lives cut short— that stench will lessen, if but briefly.

May ends in the streets,
protest marches fanning out the watershed
up and down the Gulf.
"He was a classmate of mine in high school,"
a once-college-student-of-mine messages:
One of our own has died up North,
the knee of a policeman weaponized against Big Floyd,
a sustained crushing until lungs that were always filled with song,
go limp *and the world's love and rage explode.*

"I've been out here for fifty years," an elder
with a BLACK LIVES MATTER placard

tells a young Latina reporter with a microphone.
Both speak from behind face masks.
"It is good to see the young folks here in
the streets of Corpus Christi, the body of Christ.
This is where it has to start."

We shall not, We shall not be moved.
Across the world, we people proclaim,
Black Lives Matter Everywhere!

In barrio parks and along arroyos
wherever water runs toward the sea,
a lone egret fishes. A pair of egrets
hear the drums and the dance begins anew.
We shall not, We shall not be moved.

# IX. Inside Pandemic

Chato/ Brownie/ Figueroa (every neighbor had a different name for him)
Facebook Memorial, posted March 12, 2020

He was hit at the intersection that holds memorials to his original owner.
I found out about the accident by going back to Animal Care Services Campus
once more, this morning. They looked deeper into their computer system,
found his microchip this time, and with it, the report of his death.

He was a fearless friend—
guarded his home-girl, BonnieBo, from the cars in the street when she got hit
Kept watch on my porch but barked only when necessary
Saved a wayward hen-- stepped in the way of an attacking dog,
so I could grab the bird.
I remember his quizzical response
when a passerby pulled a blade on him one day.
He didn't bark, just sort of sidestepped
away from the knife--utterly unfazed pacifist encountering
a party pooper who didn't want to play.
And that kind of de-escalation of bad-will
will be sorely missed around here, these days.
That spirit of pure, friendly optimism,
protecting our community
made me literally go to court for him last winter
stand up for our neighborhood dog,
at the risk of $1200 in fines, and,
with the presence of kindness and intelligence, win against odds.
After that we managed to neuter and microchip him.
We did not find him a home off Martin Street though.
The City said we could not have a neighborhood dog, but we did.
And if he'd lived a couple weeks longer into the stay-home, stay-safe era
I don't know what we'd done cause
he was not a socially-distancing dog. He spread goodwill to all
and often got fed for it.

Lately, he had gotten gordito
because we were trying to keep him behind my gate,
and he couldn't run & roam all day like he loved to do—
he was fine with his new collar but would not take a leash.
If you wanted him to do something he wasn't sure about,
you had to produce food.

Free spirit, Chatito, Presente! ¡Descanse en Paz!
He was never my dog, but I love him.

An Abundance of Wisdom

In the early days it was
an "Abundance of Caution"
that guided our every hesitant new action,
that brought about closures
and cancellations,
that indicated a vague something novel
besides the virus, trying to do right with
a feeling of the unknown and perhaps unprecedented
coming on in midst of naysayers who too often led-- astray.

At the Rinconcito, I pull weeds and stray grass
from among the wildflowers in the native plant plot—
I take the greenest home to feed chickens
and scatter the rest as mulch.
I water when the sky doesn't.
And I pick the juiciest oranges that are
on the part of the tree that is inside the fence—
the ones nobody who can get to them seems to want.

In the early days at the Rinconcito,
 a banner appeared on the chain link gate
that says it best, says it without the euphemisms
and lies that may yet lead to sharper disease curves upward,
"MUJER ARTES STUDIO is closed in abundance of corona virus."

Rationing, Rationalizing, Pandemic Panic

When I get the email to dress up and make things look snazzy
for our zoomed-up poetry-month reading, I scoff.
For years, I've taught online, asynchronously, as it is,
as is, since pre-pandemic times.
I don't have time for fancy cloths to do my work well
and no one has cared to keep up my contingent faculty home office.
I live in damage control mode already. I am pandemic-prepared, Covid ready.

But as the poetry day nears, I acquiesce. I decide on alizarin cochineal lip paint
offered by insects on the nopal pads that feed the neighborhood
with tender nopalitos.

I am happy that last week the 24th Street Dentist finally met me at her locked door
with hand sanitizer, let me slip in—face covered, took my temperature twice,
and, after months of waiting, mounted the permanent cap on my dental implant.
No waves of insecurity as I form a tight smile.
No visible gaps in my mouth as I shape my words with expressive gesture.

I put a Kashmiri shawl, gifted by a South Indian UIW student,
sadly now long out of touch,
over the white row-cover that curtains my windows
with a heat-catching white glow.

I put a Diego Rivera mural print on an easel behind the Amish-made, cedar rocker
where I sit at my laptop. I arrange it so the scene hides the clutter I cannot get to
in the last week of a semester guided by the compass of my crises policies.
I can tell the mural scene was painted long ago
(or in the past month) because blue mountains rise
clearly on the horizon above the cityscape.
I am comforted but haunted by the lack of social distance
in the frenzy of the crowds of people.
I embrace irony and pray she does not have the virus.

Now, as the zoom hour looms near,
my laptop and iPhone charging,
I wonder, what to wear?

And how to block the dog's bark, the cars doing their own loud zooming,
the neighbor's AC, on again, now 24/7.
Even the incessant mockingbird insistent that his voice be heard above all—
Certainly, he will set out to out-do my poetry.

I thrive on juxtapositions even when there is no pandemic intensifying them
so I worry now that I am powered by weeks' (turned months') long adrenalin drips
that will surely drain out if I don't ration them like my last toilet paper roll.

Decree

Coronavirus
crowns our society
with our inequities.
Our injustices sparkle.

Pregnancy is a vulnerability
in these times of COVID 19.
Waiving the laws that protect us
endangers all of us.
Empirically, we will see
more young women suffer,
maybe die—
        More women of color
                More women with less
                      economic means.

We will see women lose their rights
to birth a healthy child
in healthier times.

But beyond the empirical
the governor's decree against abortion
Sanctions misogyny
Sanctions injustice
Sanctions the retreat of liberty
Sanctions the isms we SHALL abolish
with the virus.

Social Bubbling

Happily alone, with a few cats and a dog,
I've never hugged and kissed so much in a single day--
Well, not for a long time--
until the news that a tiger has gotten COVID 19 from her keeper.
I pamper my companions with healthy food,
hoping we can build herd immunity together.

Nopalitos- gatherers wave at me from down the street.
They know me through the pads that burst out overnight
in my front yard to make food for all.
I offer bags for their harvest across the wrought iron gate.

My dad calls from Kansas with weather reports
that seem to shadow ours in San Antonio, (or ours, theirs, occasionally)
albeit usually much warmer here and windier there.
He reads meteorologists' forecasts ten days out,
and calculates when planting Spring crops
will be rewarded with rainfall, but hopefully not hail.
The last two years November froze, and December warmed up.
March was warm and April turned out harsh cold spells—
Even brought snow mounding on the mulch my dad and aunt
heaped over seedling beans and potatoes that kept warm within.

My dad remarks on the spikes in temperature—
40, 50, now 60 degree shifts in a few hours are not uncommon.
Last year he tried to save the peaches and apricots in full bloom
during a late Spring freeze.
He got up in early a.m. when the temperature was dropping to 32
to hover at freezing until the sun would warm the air
and he went out with a garden hose to moisten-warm
the air around blossom-laden branches.
15 minutes spraying, then he'd come in
--15 minutes to warm himself up.
From 4 a.m. to 8 a.m. he worked that way.

"I may have made it worse" he had said the next day
"but only time and careful observation will tell."

This year we fret over the weather as usual but on the News
the frenzy we feel over climate chaos has been replaced
by the attention we pay to the virus that may attack any of us,
do to us what we have done to earth, water and air.

Meadowlark: Phone Notes

Meadowlark is the perfect place
to self-isolate, he says.
And I imagine from pre-pandemic knowledge that is so.
The refuge that my grandma built was always
potentially peaceful that way
even when bustling with folks.

I am out here with the cats and the peahen
working on the mowers
working off problems,
keeping up my daily dose of sanity in the sunshine.

The next week, he reports

I was out mowing out behind the northeast side of the building
and there was a mass of bees the size of a large pizza.
I had noticed them coming up to drink from a couple old coolers
that filled up with rainwater.
The bees found their way in through lids bumped ajar.

"A swarm," I say, delighted.
Perhaps they are the returning progeny
of the bees that made honey in the wall
of our prairie barn that burned.
My mind is buzzing. My dad kept bees when I was young.
I'd tried to attract the bees in the barn to a hive to little avail.
"We must find a beehive."
Set it aways a way from the building though.
Out near the wheat and beans field perhaps,
Unless the farmer's chemicals might kill.
Or by the pond. I mowed the trash trees last fall
and the phlox are in full bloom, already

I listen, and I think
even in the midst of the corona pandemic, this land, her dream,
the reciprocity of Meadowlark homestead these days
would make Grandma smile.

My Diary (Yet to be Named): Found Poem from the 1918 Pandemic*

I am going to put [my diary] in a box and perhaps some little girl a long, long time from now will find [it] there and read...

I have decided to give this diary a name. Then I can call it something. I don't know what yet.
We live on Washburn College Campus. We have five rooms of an apartment house. It makes it a lot easier for mama not to have to bother with the old coal as the heat is furnished. There are just lots of trees and birds. There are lots of smooth wide sidewalks for me to skate on too.

Here it is fall again. School has begun but we are going to be out for a week on account of the Spanish Influenza. All the schools and public houses are closed all over Kansas. We just lay around and do nothing because there's nothing to do. Not even any church or S.S....

Friday, October 25.
We have guards on campus at night. It's awfully thrilling. One went right up and down under our bedroom window one night and we heard him say "Halt! Who goes there?" [N]ow since "the flue" has been here the campus is in quarantine. *Guards all the time night and day to keep people from going in or out <u>and we can't go off the campus.</u> Mama has a pass. I think I will have to get one to take... my music lesson. We see some of the choicest things and mind you I was just walking from our house over to the Observatory and a guard called out halt. I halted and told him where I was going and where I came from. He said he had orders not to allow any girls to go into any of the buildings on account of "the flue" So he had to call the Corporal of the Guard to let me by.... The Corporal let me by but he said the guard had orders to halt everyone. It was sure funny. Dorothy comes and talks to me over the stone wall. Sunday was the first time they had the guard on in the daytime. Folks always come to walk on the campus on Sunday. It was a perfect circus to watch the guards turn folks back. Automobiles too. All the faculty folks have passes. I don't know what possessed me not to speak about my birthday when it came. It is on May the 12th. I was 13. It is pretty near Christmas again.*

Monday, October 28.
Saturday and Sunday it rained all the time and they didn't have the guards out cause they might catch cold and then they would get "the flue." It was kind of cold this morning and we thought maybe the quarantine *was over so I was planning to go to the store and we thought we'd go walking in the meadow. But this morning the guards were on as usual. We took advantage of the rain Saturday and Sunday and saw a great deal of the outer world. I felt like a bird just out of its cage when I stepped outside of the wall.*

*Found poem from the diary of Ruth Platt, 13 years old in 1918. Thanks to Zona Galle for keeping and sharing the diary.

"Honk, it's my birthday!"

proclaimed in bold color on poster board mounted by the street.
and do they ever *honk*—a vehicular parade that lasts hours--
cars caravan,
motorcycle motorcade,
SUV's, low-riders,
beach-ready hippy vans and repair & lawn-work ready work vans,
farm truck for transporting feria, hybrid car,
an electric bike and a Rascuache scooter contraption:
They all pass by and honk at our newly-minted-twelve-year-old neighbor—
in slim jeans and a light shirt, sleeves rolled to take on what the world offers.
She flips back her long black hair as she waves at a world welcoming her
to early adulthood.

As late April sun heaves its intense glow toward the street
still closed for construction two blocks west,
the street itself turns into a stage:
a fashion runway for celebratory, motorized Westside ingenuity
in times of pandemic.
Shrieking gales of speed, wheels whir & tires wail,
but it is brakes that blast neighborhood sound barriers.

I come out to the sidewalk, directly across the street—
with a scarf—Zapatista-tied across my face
to take my nightly photograph of the maguey
I planted over 15 years ago in my front yard that now has shot up a huge stalk,
soon to hold a chandelier of blossoms.
This evening, three baby arms with tiny fingers have emerged at the top.
I almost squeal in delight.
I know the blooming will mark the end of the maguey's life.
I had hoped for more time,
but I understand the timing it, or the universe, chose.
An era is ending with this pandemic.
The maguey's progeny, shelter in place all around its easily 13-foot circumference.
We will nurture the new plants.
Our duty now is to celebrate.

… Impending

Volatilities

The fires came on the heels of drought and heat,
iron heels clasping August earth in jaws
composed of more manmade materials
than what lurks in the uppers of cheap shoes.
They sear the edges of the seasons
and Nature's torture forces confessions
made in desperation and without sincerity
signaling to the seers
that another year
will intensify this hot plague
until even the soil will burn without cause.
Even the air will ignite
should we dare whisper
the wrong passion, arouse embers,
and stir up dormant emotions,
like the hurricanes
stirred dry winds from the Gulf
that churned into fires,
burned Bastrop's brushy hills,
burned the pines of Pedernales
and keepsakes stored in attic chests
that had arrived in the hill country
100 years before the last great drought of '56.
The fires burned at the edges of bones
buried in the shadow of nopal
where I had passed through
on Monday driving south to school,
and having driven already many hundred miles
I barely noticed the familiar scenery
though I remember thinking I'd never seen the land so dry.
I barely noticed the familiar that will never be seen again--
except as recorded on film (or, more likely now, digital image)
before the burn—
the landscape that I passed through so quickly

and now regret,
as if my dawdling could have kept the fires at bay
could have stilled the wind
or lowered the heat
or brought the rain.

Flamenco for the Earth,

What can humans do to reverse the throes of earth's illnesses?
How have our unbridled energies caused them?
How does our chaos condense into the tornado's swirling fervor?
the fire's catapulting flames?
the torrents inundating earth in sheer randomness?
What can human dancers do to reverse throes of earth's demise?
What can human choirs do, but sing with all gusto
left in our bodies,
passion muscling against emptying flesh,
bones clattering into collapse?

What can we do to discipline our climatic delinquency,
but stomp and twirl and throw ourselves
into the last, great, frenzied dance?

If earth shall go extinct
in wake of rising gases,
we manufacture,
we can surely pause,
take silent stock of the furor
of what is sweeping us away
all we stand to lose,
have lost,

and then resume the dance
that will never give rise to music
in our children's times.

Something, Ending
"God is gender free." Amalia Ortiz

"I can't breathe, mama, mama" he called out.
anima mundi, universal soul has answered
with planetary wounds,
marks on our own hands & feet.

Now Let Us Shift

Prometheus Corona
Her crown draped with a face mask
will not save, condone or condemn us.

We move to save earth
from ourselves,
bring fire to the night—birth seeds
foreshadow the darkest of the earth to shine Black.

My maguey blooms, and its muscles droop,
sculptural leaves evaporate,
give water-life to the blossoms, then black seeds,
and to the tangle of pups, babies growing at her base.

We/they had it wrong with light white supremacy
we are blinded like the man, on the road to kill.
Sight returns on the third day, with dusk.

I am the other you
You are the other me.

We are not separate,
but YinYang, enjoined-- silverized
by beating, pumping, breathing.
Hapi, Maize-Moon Goddexx, Great Manitou

Energy is motion
and then in rest.

Mother Earth Pursues America's 19th Amendment

In the aftermath of a great pandemic
that scourged our nation
100 years back in the month of Leo
In the heartland of August—Canícula
the nation ratified the rights of all women to vote.
Following the struggle of women of all colors and creeds
men conceded to their humanity and wisdom.
The 19th Amendment caught the eye of Mother Earth
in her place at the center of our Universe.
She made plans to vote, herself.
Her citizenship was grandmothered—she is the greatest grandmother
after all, Mother Earth preceded all—predated all borders on earth-- slavery,
Doctrine of Discovery, and racist voting laws.
She exists before and beyond pi r-squared.
So Mother Earth filled in a vote-by-mail form
and sent it out across the universe
to the east shore of Turtle Island,
the up and coming 51st state, Douglass Commonwealth.

Men paid no heed,
nor did the women who had joined them
slowly in the halls of Congress.
100 years passed
and nevertheless, Mother Earth persisted.
Mother Earth 2020 still campaigns
for her universal rights
to have voice in all the nations
who have not yet declared Earth,
hers, to speak for.
In the 21st Century pandemic USA
Women still struggle
for equal pay for equal work.
We play catch-up with other nations—
we have not yet inaugurated a woman to our helm,

we have yet to give all, equal access to the vote.
When we slow the curve of our 2019+ pandemic
on the centenary of women's right to vote
may we join those nations
who have given voice to the rights of Mother Earth.
May her vote guide all nations to equilibrium.

About the Author

Kamala Platt, Ph.D., MFA is an author, artist, independent scholar and contingent professor living in South Texas and at The Meadowlark Center, Kansas. She currently teaches creative writing, Chicana Poetry, Environmental Justice Poetics and Pen Project Prison Teaching for the School of Humanities, Arts and Cultural Studies in Arizona State University's Online Program. She has shared her visual art and poetry widely, often in community arts and cultural centers and at conferences. Last year's highlight exhibit was "Bird Island Photo Diptich: I. Summer Pachanga & II. Halcyon Hellscape after Advent Attacks" in *"Emotional Numbness: The impact of war on the human psyche and ecosystems"* at Platform 3, Tehran, Iran, and Online, July 2020 – January 2021. She also participated in Zoom poetry readings in conjunction with Stone in the Stream, Sierra Club, Bihl Haus, and more.

Through "green rascuache" lifeways, Kamala searches borderlands for footholds of dignity & well-being (resistance to walls, injustices, militarisms, 'isms, ecological disrespect...) amidst a feverish planet's crises. Her current scholarship shares women's environmental justice poetics creating a lens through which to understand visions of a "sustainable" future. She is preparing her manuscript *Environmental Justice Poetics: Cultural Representations of Environmental Racism from Chicanas and Women in India* for publication with De Gruyter in Berlin.

Her Westside Barrio, San Antonio home and nearby "Garden of Good Trouble" host native habitat, garden, and orchard offering seasonal produce: limones, loquats, nopalitos, tunas, figs, and pomegranites to share; a library and studio hold books & art. Family roots in ecology and human rights and a cross-cultural childhood among Mennonites in Kansas, & family friends/coworkers in Orissa (Odisha), India, provides foundation. In recent years, Fuerza Unida, Esperanza Center for Peace & Justice, Texas Master Naturalists, Cultural Capital, Climate Reality Leadership and Texas Women Farmers' Holistic Management and Native Plant, Bonsai, and Cactus & Xerophyte groups have built her knowledge and she currently works in solidarity with groups supporting immigrants and other marginalized and displaced communities including SA Stands, and San Antonio Coalition for Police Accountability.

Kamala has held fellowships with Center for the Study of Women and

Society, OU (Women, Science & the Sacred), Feminist Research Institute (UNM) and the Guadalupe Cultural Arts Center (Gateways) in San Antonio. She holds an MFA in poetry (BGSU, Ohio), an MA in Interdisciplinary Arts (Columbia College, Chicago), a Ph.D. in Comparative Literature (UT, Austin) and an undergraduate degree (Art, International Development, Religion), Bethel College, Kansas.

Publications: Creative Writing Manuscripts
Weedslovers: Ten Years in the Shadow of September, (Poetry) Finishing Line Press, March, 2014.
On the Line. (Poetry) Wings Press, March 1, 2010. 128 pgs.
Kinientos: New Pictures of an Old World An Anthology Commemorating the Past 500 Years. Compiled with Dani Apodaca & Alli Aweusi, Wordsworth, October 1992.
Making Do With Unrequited Love in Times of Terror. trans-genre collection in progress.